Ancient Hymns From the Roman Breviary

ANCIENT HYMNS, Etc.

RIVINGTONS

London	Waterloo Place
Oxford	High Street
Cambridge	Trinity Street

NCIENT HYMNS

From the Roman Breviary

TO WHICH ARE ADDED

ORIGINAL HYMNS

BY RICHARD MANT, D.D.

SOMETIME LORD BISHOP OF DOWN AND CONNOR

RIVINGTONS

London, Oxford, and Cambridge

1871

(New Edition)

Contents.

I. MORNING AND EVENING HYMNS FOR EACH DAY IN THE WEEK

FIRST SERIES

II. MORNING AND EVENING HYMNS FOR EACH

DAY IN THE WEEK

SECOND SERIES

III. HYMNS FOR OUR LORD'S HOLY DAYS

IV. HYMNS FOR SAINTS' DAYS

ix

* From the Parisian Breviary.

ORIGINAL HYMNS

PRINCIPALLY OF

COMMEMORATION AND THANKSGIVING FOR CHRIST'S HOLY ORDINANCES

* From the Author's ' Holy Days of the Church.'

I

Morning and Evening Hymns

FOR EACH DAY IN THE WEEK

FIRST SERIES

A

Morning Hymn for Sunday

Primo die quo Trinitas

On this first day, when heaven and earth
Rose at the Triune's word to birth;
The day when He, who gave us breath,
Revived our souls and vanquish'd death;

Why close in sleep your languid eyes?
Shake off dull slumber, wake, arise;
And, mindful of the Prophet's voice,
Right early in our God rejoice.

That He may hear the ascending cry;
That He may stretch His hand from high;
That He may cleanse, and make us meet
To join Him in yon heavenly seat:

That, while each consecrated hour
We praise and sing His glorious power,
The offerings of this day of rest
May with His choicest gifts be blest.

Paternal Glory, Sire of all,
Thee with o'erflowing hearts we call,
That we this day may serve Thee, freed
From guilty thought and sinful deed :

That no foul passion's lawless flame
May injure this corporeal frame ;
Nor the unhallow'd heart's desire
Plunge us in flames of fiercer fire.

Saviour of men, whose blood alone
Can for a ruin'd world atone,
Cleanse Thou our hearts, and upward lift
To share in Thy perennial gift.

5

To Thee, most Holy Sire ; to Thee,
Co-equal only Son, we flee :
With Him, the union to complete,
The Spirit blest, the Paraclete.

II

Evening Hymn for Sunday

Lucis Creator Optime

O THOU, of light Creator best,
Who didst the days with light invest;
And bid its new-born radiance shine
To glad creation's origin:

Thou, who the morn to evening join'd
For day's formation hast assign'd;
Lo, round us spreads a gloomy shade,
Thy suppliants hear, their sorrows aid!

The soul, in sin's hard bondage held,
Oh, be she not from life expell'd;
While yet to things eternal blind,
In bands of wilful guilt confined.

7

Grant to heaven's portal she may rise,
And claim the everlasting prize ;
But first, from sin's oppression free,
Grant her on earth to walk with Thee !

Such favour, Lord, of Thee we pray,
Thy blessing on this closing day ;
Sole Sovereign of the heavenly host,
Thee Father, Son, and Holy Ghost.

III

Morning Hymn for Monday

Jam lucis orto sidere

BRIGHTLY shines the morning-star :
　Pray we God His grace to give,
That from sin and danger far
　We the coming day may live.

That the tongue, by Him withheld,
　May from sounds of strife refrain ;
That the eye, from roving quell'd,
　Seek not sights corrupt or vain :

That the heart, with pureness fraught,
　May from folly turn aside ;
And the flesh, by temperance taught,
　Calm its lusts, and veil its pride :

That, when He the day shall close,
  And the night successive bring,
We, triumphant o'er our foes,
  May our hymn of glory sing ;

Glory, Sire of all, to Thee ;
  And to Thee, Co-equal Son,
With the Spirit, glory be ;
  One in Three, and Three in One.

IV

Evening Hymn for Monday

Immense cæli Conditor

ALL-PRESENT Framer of the sky,
Who spread'st the firmament on high,
And badest the parted waters flow,
The broad expanse above, below ;

Each to the space, for each assign'd,
By Thee in heaven and earth confined,
The heats by moisture to allay,
Lest earth's parch'd soil they waste away :

Pour out Thy Spirit, and embue
Our hearts with Thy perpetual dew ;
Lest the deep taint of early time
Wear out the soul with recent crime.

Let Faith her growing light supply,
A sunbeam to the clouded eye ;
O'er falsehood's mists exalt her head,
And on the world's vain follies tread.

So be Thy will, O Father, done ;
And Thine, Co-equal only Son ;
With Him combined in union meet,
The Holy Ghost, the Paraclete.

V

Morning Hymn for Tuesday

Ales diei nuntius

THE bird, the harbinger of light,
　Has sung his morning strain :
Hear ye not Christ our minds excite,
　And call to life again ?

'Arise,' He cries, 'your beds forsake,
　Nor slothful, slumbering, lie !
Chaste, upright, temperate, wake, awake ;
　For I, behold, am nigh.'

With prayer, and praise, and minds sedate
　We, too, the Saviour rouse :
For holy hearts delight to wait
　On God with holy vows.

Do Thou, O Christ, our souls awake,
  Burst Thou the chains of night ;
Of ancient sin the bondage break,
  And shine with new-form'd light !

To God the Father be addrest,
  And to the only Son,
All glory, with the Spirit blest,
  Eternal Three in One !

VI

Evening Hymn for Tuesday

Telluris alme Conditor

ALL-BOUNTEOUS Framer of the earth,
Thou who the seas, her kindred birth,
Didst drive apart ; and give to stand
High o'er the flood the solid land :

That thence might spring the tender shoot,
The colour'd flower, the pleasant fruit ;
The grass, her future tribes to feed ;
And, wrapt in each, its genial seed :

The wounds of the diseased soul
Make thou with gracious freshness whole :
That she her sins in tears may steep,
Her lusts in due subjection keep ;

To Thy commands allegiance pay ;
From all that's evil turn away ;
At all that's good with pleasure glow ;
Nor the keen sting of dying know.

So be Thy will, O Father, done ;
And Thine, Co-equal only Son ;
And Thine, who sharest the imperial seat,
Spirit of life, blest Paraclete.

VII

𝔐orning 𝔥ymn for 𝔚ednesday

Consors paterni luminis

CONSORT of paternal light,
  Light of Light, essential day,
Bidding farewell to the night,
  Lo ! to Thee we sing and pray.

Chase the darkness from the mind,
  Chase the powers of night afar ;
Let not sleep our senses bind,
  Nor the sluggish spirit mar.

Christ, behold with kind regard,
  What to Thee in faith we bear ;
Let the morning hymn be heard,
  Herald to the morning prayer.

Prayer and hymn receive, addrest
    To Thy Father, and to Thee,
And Thy Holy Spirit blest,
    Reigning to eternity.

VIII

Evening Hymn for Wednesday

Cæli Deus sanctissime

THRICE Holy Sovereign of the sky,
Who o'er the lucid tracts on high
Thy fleecy brightness dost diffuse,
And paint them with thy beauteous hues :

Thou who along the expanse of air
Didst wheel the sun's refulgent car,
Ordain the moon's perpetual course,
And curb the planets' wandering force :

Apt in their motions to divide
The morning from the evening tide ;
And by each season's noted sign
The days, and months, and years define :

Our darken'd hearts illume with day,
Our souls' defilements purge away,
The band of conscious guilt unbind,
And lighten the sin-burden'd mind.

Such favour, Lord, of Thee we pray,
Thy blessing on this closing day,
Sole Sovereign of the heavenly host,
Thee Father, Son, and Holy Ghost.

IX

Morning Hymn for Thursday

Æterna cœli gloria

O ETERNAL praise of heaven,
Blessed Hope to mortals given,
Partner of the Father's throne,
Thou the Virgin-born alone ;

Grant us, as from sleep we rise,
Healthful thoughts to scale the skies,
And to God with ardour raise
Due return of thankful praise.

By the star of morning led,
Lifts the sun his orient head :
Rescued from the gloom of night,
Lighten us with holy light.

Grant it in our hearts to dwell,
Thence the world's dark shades expel ;
And through each succeeding time
Cleanse our breasts from taint of crime.

There may Faith first strike her root,
Hope, with joy's delightful fruit,
And, the greatest of the three,
Thine own handmaid, Charity.

Hymning thus our matin lay,
Son of God, to Thee we pray ;
And join with Thine through endless days
The Father's and the Spirit's praise.

X

Evening Hymn for Thursday

Magnæ Deus potentiæ

God of all nature, great and good,
Who gavest the flood-engender'd brood,
Some in their liquid bed to lie,
And some to soar the lofty sky ;

Form'd or beneath the wave to swim,
Or the thin air uplifted skim,
Sprung from one stock, each varied race
Fills his appointed dwelling-place.

Meet grace to all Thy servants show ;
Be theirs no lapse of guilt to know,
Cleansed by the blood, salvation's spring,
Nor bear of death the lingering sting.

Be none deprest by wilful fault,
Let none vain-glorious thoughts exalt,
Lest the weak mind, destruction's thrall,
O'erburden'd sink, o'ervaulting fall.

So be Thy will, Great Father, done,
And Thine, the well-beloved Son ;
And Thine, who reign'st in union meet,
Spirit of life, blest Paraclete.

XI

Morning Hymn for Friday

Splendor Paternæ Gloriæ

IMAGE of the Father's might,
  Of His light essential ray,
Source of splendour, Light of light,
  Day that dost illume the day ;
Shining with unsullied beam,
Sun of truth, descending stream ;
And upon our clouded sense
Pour thy Spirit's influence.

Father, Thee too we implore ;
  Father, of almighty grace ;
Father, of eternal power ;
  Taint of sin from us efface.

Each innocuous act advance,
Turn to good each evil chance,
Blunt the sting of envy's tooth,
Keep us in the ways of truth.

Rule our minds, our actions form,
  Cleanse our hearts with chastity,
Give us love sincere and warm,
  Uprightness from falsehood free.
Christ, our living spring and meat,
Freely let us drink and eat ;
And our gladden'd souls embue
With the Spirit's healthful dew.

Joy be ours the passing day,
  Pureness like the morning's glow,
Faith as clear as noontide ray,
  May the mind no twilight know.

26

Welcoming the dawning bright,
Thus we pray a holier light,
From the eternal Fountain drawn,
On our waken'd souls may dawn.

XII

Evening Hymn for Friday

Hominis superne Conditor

FATHER of men, whose sovereign will
Thy works, ordain'd by Thee, fulfil;
Who badest the earth to being bring
Cattle, and beast, and creeping thing;

And, as to life call'd forth by Thee,
Those mighty forms began to be,
Badest them, as time should onward roll,
Obey Thy favour'd man's control:

Do Thou the impulse strong defeat,
If lawless lust our steps beset,
Or thought of inward evil breed,
Or mingle with the outward deed.

Do Thou Thy promised blessings give,
Grant us beneath Thy grace to live ;
Dissension's hateful bands unbind,
And stablish peace with all mankind.

Such favour, Lord, of Thee we pray,
Thy blessing on this closing day,
Sole Sovereign of the heavenly host,
Thee Father, Son, and Holy Ghost.

XIII

Morning Hymn for Saturday

Nox et tenebræ et nubila

Lo, night and clouds and darkness wrapp'd
  The world in dense array,
The morning dawns, the light breaks forth,
  Hence, hence, ye shades, away.
Pierced by the sun's resistless shafts
  Disparts the embattled gloom,
And all things, lighten'd by his face,
  Their wonted hues resume.

Thee, Christ, our only hope, we seek,
  With meek and simple heart,
With prayers and hymns that Thou wilt deign
  Thy daily grace impart:

Dark is the soul, and needs Thy light,
  To make her pure and clean ;
That light, which shines in heaven, show forth,
  And smile with face serene.

So may our minds the radiant beams
  Of Thy enlightening know ;
So may our hearts by Thee inflamed
  With holy transport glow ;
So may our tongues, inspired by Thee,
  Still sing the Eternal One ;
The Father, and the Holy Ghost,
  With Thee, begotten Son.

XIV

Evening Hymn for Saturday

Jam Sol recedit igneus

Now sinks in night the flaming sun :
  O Thou, our everlasting day,
Thrice holy Godhead, Three in One,
    Thy brightness to our hearts display :
To Thee we hymn the morning lay,
    To Thee our evening vows are given ;
Grant us, as here to Thee we pray,
    To praise Thee in the courts of heaven.

No shadows there nor clouds impede
  The view with visions of affright :
Nor sun nor moon those mansions need,
  The Lamb is their perpetual light.

Oh, yet unseen by mortal sight,
  May in our souls that scene endure,
That we, through hope of that delight,
  May purer grow as Thou art pure.

And when the day shall come, that we
  Shall know no more, as now, in part,
May we unveiled Thy presence see,
  Be like, and know Thee as Thou art :
And evermore with voice and heart
  Join concert with Thy heavenly host,
And bear, in praising Thee, our part,
  Thee Father, Son, and Holy Ghost.

II

Morning and Evening Hymns

FOR EACH DAY IN THE WEEK

SECOND SERIES.

C

XV

Morning Hymn for Sunday

O Sol salutis intimis

SALVATION'S Sun, the inward gloom
That veils our hearts, do Thou illume :
Now that the night is driven away,
And lovelier shines this holy day.

Behold, the accepted time is here !
Grant us to wash with contrite tear
The heart's vow'd offering, and above
Present it on the fire of love.

The fount, which wont with sin to teem,
Shall weep with grief a living stream,
If the hard rock's reluctant side
Repentance' potent rod divide.

The day, Thine own blest day, appears,
When a fresh bloom all nature wears ;
And we, whom Thy right hand and voice
Now guide aright, may we rejoice !

May the world's transitory frame,
All-bounteous Triad, bless Thy Name ;
And, by Thy grace renew'd, may we
New songs of glory sing to Thee.

To Thee, whose name, as heretofore,
Now and for ever shall adore
Thy Church on earth, Thy heavenly host,
Thee Father, Son, and Holy Ghost.

XVI

Evening Hymn for Sunday

[ORIGINAL]

THE day declines : but, ere it part,
The day that glads the Christian's heart,
For all the good, its course conveys,
Sing we to God our evening praise.

Praise Him, that we this day have trod
With reverent feet the house of God ;
Our sins with lowly hearts confest,
And by His pardoning word been blest.

Praise Him, that we have sought Him there
By His commission'd minister ;
And, kneeling at His mercy's throne,
Have made our wants and wishes known.

Praise Him, that we have raised our voice
In our Salvation to rejoice,
And blest His name, His Church among,
In psalm, and hymn, and holy song.

Praise Him, that we this day have heard
The truths of His most holy word :
Which leads us, prone, alas ! to stray,
Thro' earth's dark snares the heavenward way.

Praise Him, that we our thanks have paid
For blessings to mankind display'd ;
For all the good this life can prove,
But most for His redeeming love.

Praise Him, that thus we've sought His face,
His day by His own means of grace :
Praise Him for night's approaching rest,
Praise Father, Son, and Spirit blest.

XVII

Morning Hymn for Monday

Nocte surgentes vigilemus omnes, etc.
Ecce jam noctis tenuatur umbra, etc.

AWAKING with the waken'd day,
  The morning anthem raise ;
And to our God the tribute pay,
  The hymn of tuneful praise.

O may the theme our souls prepare
  To join the angels' throng ;
And sing with them our Maker there
  In never-ending song.

Away the night and darkness fly,
  Light brightens in the east ;
Hear, Lord of all, our suppliant cry,
  To Thee in faith addrest.

Our souls o'erspent with guilt release,
  Our load of sin forgive ;
And grant us evermore in peace
  And health with Thee to live.

Paternal Godhead, hear the hymn,
  And grant the meek request,
With Him, Thy Glory's Filial Beam,
  And Him, the Spirit blest.

XVIII

Evening Hymn for Monday

Rector potens, verax Deus

MIGHTY Sovereign, God supreme,
　　Ruler of the varied day,
Who send'st forth the morning beam,
　　Whom the noontide heats obey ;

Who the hours, as on they glide,
　　Givest, to Thee as seemeth best,
And the peaceful eventide
　　Hast ordain'd for welcome rest:

Quench dissension's baneful fire,
　　Bid each noxious heat depart,
To our bodies health inspire,
　　Peace and comfort to the heart.

To Thy care Thy servants take,
From all nightly ills preserve ;
That to-morrow we may wake,
Thee with strength renew'd to serve.

Holy Father, grant our prayer,
Grant it, sole co-equal Son,
Grant it, blessed Comforter,
One in Three, and Three in One.

XIX

𝕸orning 𝕳ymn for 𝕿uesday

Somno refectis artubus

OUR limbs refresh'd with wholesome sleep,
We scorn the bed of sloth to keep,
But rise, and Thee, our Father, pray,
To hear and bless our morning lay.

To Thee the voice be first addrest,
By Thee the waking thought possest,
That each succeeding act may be
Commenced, pursued, fulfill'd in Thee !

Now darkness fades before the light,
Yields to the dawn the gloom of night ;
If aught of ill the night conceal'd,
So may it to Thy brightness yield.

44

O grant that thus our hearts within
May still be clean from taint of sin ;
And still our outward lips may raise
To Thee the voice of deathless praise.

So be Thy will, Great Father, done ;
And Thine, the Father's only Son ;
And Thine, who sharest the imperial seat,
Spirit of life, blest Paraclete !

xx

Evening Hymn for Tuesday

Nox atra rerum contigit

DARK night arrays in hueless vest
  This undistinguish'd scene ;
To Thee we fly, our sins confest,
  Judge of the hearts of men.

Do Thou our former faults atone,
  Wash Thou our minds impure ;
And by Thy mercy's sovereign boon
  From guilt's assaults secure.

The soul, to conscious sin a prey,
  In unblest torpor weak :
Fain would she cast her slough away,
  And Thee, her Saviour, seek.

The gloom, but chief that gloom expel,
   Which clouds the mental sight,
That the glad soul her bliss may feel,
   And bless Thy saving light.

Such grace, Eternal One in Three,
   We seek this hour of rest,
Of Thee, O Father; Son, of Thee ;
   And Thee, O Spirit blest !

XXI

Morning Hymn for Wednesday

Lux ecce surgit aurea

BEHOLD, it shines, the golden light!
Haste, waning shadows, haste your flight;
That we, through danger's devious way,
No more may blindly, darkly, stray.

Shine, blessed light, serenely shine,
And show our brightness pure as thine;
Obscured in lips or heart by naught
Of crafty word, or fraudful thought.

So pass the day entire along;
Nor treacherous hand, nor lying tongue,
Nor roving eyes, betray to sin
The outward form or soul within.

See from above the watchman's eye !
To Him our days all open lie :
By Him are all our deeds survey'd,
From opening dawn to evening shade.

And so to Him be praise addrest,
To Father, Son, and Spirit blest,
Now, as it was through ages past,
And shall through endless ages last.

XXII

Evening Hymn for Wednesday

Rerum Deus tenax vigor

NATURE'S God, all-ruling Power,
  Who, Thyself exempt from change,
Dost for each successive hour
  Its diurnal course arrange :
Cheer our darkness with Thy light,
Succour us the approaching night,
From our homes all perils keep,
Nourish us with wholesome sleep.

Lord, my spirit to Thy care,
  Sleeping, waking, I commend :
Thou canst its decays repair,
  Thou from injury defend.

D

Grant me life, if life Thou will,
Thy commandments to fulfil ;
Or, if death be Thy decree,
Grant me such as leads to Thee.

Living, dead, Thy succour give,
   Grant me, Lord, Thy saving grace ;
Living, still with Thee to live,
   Dead, that I may see Thy face ;
Evermore with Thee to dwell,
Evermore Thy praise to tell,
Singing with Thy heavenly host
Father, Son, and Holy Ghost.

XXIII

Morning Hymn for Thursday

Æterne rerum Conditor

MAKER of all, enthroned above,
  Whose laws the day and night arrange,
And cause the seasons round to move,
  Ordain'd in grateful interchange ;

Soon as the morn's enlightening ray
  Calls on the slumbering world to wake,
The lurking tribes, that roam'd for prey,
  Their haunts of wickedness forsake :

Smooth o'er the waves to glide is seen,
  With new-strung force the seaman's bark ;
And, holding on her course serene,
  Hails the fresh light the Church's ark.

O Jesus, Sun of righteousness,
  Do Thou thy cloudless face reveal;
'T is Thine the darken'd soul to bless,
  'T is Thine the ills of night to heal.

The lapse of sin do Thou repair,
  With renovating lustre shine :
Thine be the early morning prayer,
  The morning hymn of glory Thine !

Glory, incarnate Son, to Thee,
  The life and light of men confest ;
And, join'd in trinal unity,
  Thy Sire supreme, Thy Spirit blest !

XXIV

Evening Hymn for Thursday

Te lucis ante terminum

ERE the waning light decay,
God of all, to Thee we pray,
Thee Thy healthful grace to send,
Thee to guard us and defend.

Guard from dreams that may affright ;
Guard from terrors of the night ;
Guard from foes, without, within ;
Outward danger, inward sin.

Mindful of our only stay,
Duly thus to Thee we pray ;
Duly thus to Thee we raise
Trophies of our grateful praise.

54

Hear the prayer, Almighty King !
Hear Thy praises while we sing,
Hymning with Thy heavenly host,
Father, Son, and Holy Ghost.

XXV

Morning Hymn for Friday

Aurora jam spargit polum

WITH dawn's faint streaks the heaven is sown,
 O'er earth glides on the day,
Abroad the shafts of light are thrown,
 Hence, vain deceits, away !

Away, each phantom of the night,
 Dread of the conscious sense :
Whate'er of fault hath lent affright
 To gloomy darkness, hence !

That the last morn each gloomy shade,
 Which here we pray to shun,
Quench'd in that glorious light may fade,
 Before that cloudless sun :

While purged from sin, that o'er the sight
  Now throws its shadows dim,
We walk abroad in heaven's pure light,
  And chant our thankful hymn.

All Glory to the Eternal One
  Be evermore addrest,
To God, the Father, and the Son,
  Joined with the Spirit blest.

XXVI

Evening Hymn for Friday

Æterne Rector siderum

ALMIGHTY God, whose sceptre sways
  The earth and starry sky,
Whose will the world beneath obeys,
  Nor less the world on high :

In order meet about Thy throne
  Unnumber'd angels stand,
Prepared where'er Thou wilt to run,
  And act by Thy command.

O from that host of heavenly powers
  Some friendly spirit send,
To watch us in our lonely hours,
  And in our sleep defend ;

To guard us from our ghostly foe,
  The serpent's subtle wile,
Lest secret fraud our steps o'erthrow,
  And specious arts beguile.

Night comes : and, wrapt in nightly shade
  Lurks many a fearful snare :
But none Thy wisdom can evade,
  And Thy protecting care.

Still be Thy care, O God, our shield ;
  Still may thy wisdom guide
Us, whom Thy Holy Ghost has seal'd
  For whom Thy Son has died.

XXVII

𝕸𝖔𝖗𝖓𝖎𝖓𝖌 𝕳𝖞𝖒𝖓 𝖋𝖔𝖗 𝕾𝖆𝖙𝖚𝖗𝖉𝖆𝖞

Tu Trinitatis Unitas

HOLY Being, One and Three,
Ruler of the world, to Thee,
In this hour of morning calm,
Hark ! we chant the wakeful psalm.

Calm is yet the hour of prime ;
Hear us, mindful of the time,
Holy Being, Thee implore,
Balm on all our wounds to pour.

If this night the foe has wrought
Evil deed, or noxious thought,
Far from us the snare of hell
May Thy heavenly power repel !

May no sin our bodies stain,
May our hearts no dulness chain ;
Nor the lukewarm spirit faint,
Sickening by corruption's taint.

Rather Thou, Most Holy, shine
On our hearts with light divine ;
That each day, as round it goes,
Guiltless pass, and peaceful close :

And again at evening dim
We may wake the grateful hymn,
Ruler of the world, to Thee,
Holy Being, One and Three.

XXVIII

Evening Hymn for Saturday

[ORIGINAL]

ANOTHER day is well-nigh done,
Another week its course hath run :
But who the next, or week or day,
Shall see conclude, what tongue can say ?

Praise God for all the time He lent ;
His pardon pray for time misspent ;
And beg that we may better spend
Whate'er His bounty yet shall lend.

So, if we see the morrow's beam,
May we our former loss redeem ;
Commencing while to God we pay
The duties of that holy day.

Or, if the day, the week, that's past,
Be of our time ordain'd the last,
May our rapt souls His grace convey
To wake in His eternal day !

To Thee, in whom we live and move,
Father of comfort, God of love ;
From whom at first our being flow'd,
Thy gift, and still to Thee is owed :

To Thee, Thrice Holy, thus we raise
Our even song of prayer and praise ;
And aye our matin offering be,
Thrice Holy Being, paid to Thee !

III.

Hymns for our Lord's Holy Days.

XXIX

𝕳𝖞𝖒𝖓 𝖋𝖔𝖗 𝕬𝖇𝖇𝖊𝖓𝖙 (1.)

Verbum supernum prodiens

WORD uncreate, Beloved One,
The eternal Sire's Co-equal Son,
Who in the course mature of time
Camest forth to bless this world of crime :

Illume our minds Thy truth to see,
Our souls inflame with love of Thee,
That, spurning earth's deceitful toys,
Our hearts may soar to heavenly joys.

So when Thy dreadful doom proclaims,
' Hence, sinners, to eternal flames ;'
And milder tones the just invite
To mansions of serene delight :

E

Not ours may be the whirling storm,
The quenchless fire, the deathless worm ;
But heavenly bliss to dwell with Thee,
And God with open face to see.

All blessing, honour, glory, power,
To Him whom all His saints adore,
His Church below, His heavenly host,
To Father, Son, and Holy Ghost.

XXX

Hymn for Advent (2.)

En clara vox redarguit

HARK ! a voice of warning, hark !
Sounds it through the nations dark.
Hence, ye baseless visions, fly !
Jesus lightens from on high.

From the ground, where sunk it lies,
Let the torpid mind arise.
Banishing all evil far,
O'er us shines a new-born star.

Lo, the Lamb, before us set,
Freely cancels all our debt :
Lowly all with tears His face
Seek we, and implore His grace.

So when He shines forth again,
Striking dread in guilty men,
He may from our sins forbear
Vengeance, and in mercy spare.

Hymns of glory, notes of praise,
Through eternal ages raise,
To the Father, and the Son,
And the Spirit, Three in One.

XXXI

𝕳𝖞𝖒𝖓 𝖋𝖔𝖗 𝕺𝖚𝖗 𝕷𝖔𝖗𝖉'𝖘 𝕹𝖆𝖙𝖎𝖛𝖎𝖙𝖞 (1.)

Jesu Redemptor omnium

REDEEMER, Jesus, Life of man,
Begotten ere the light began,
Of the Paternal Light supreme,
Co-equal, co-eternal Beam :

Bright Image of the Father's mind,
Perennial Hope of all mankind,
Hear Thou the vows, by land, by sea,
Which all Thy servants pour to Thee.

Maker of all, Thy flock regard ;
And think, with us to dwell prepared,
How Thou didst once our form assume,
Born of the Virgin's holy womb.

Bear witness this auspicious morn,
Which ages past beheld Thee born,
That Thou to save us camest alone
Forth issuing from Thy Father's throne.

Him stars, and earth, the wat'ry main,
Him all that heaven's broad belts contain,
That new salvation's Author praise,
With welcoming of new-made lays.

And we, for whom thy holy blood
Has pour'd a sanctifying flood,
To Thee, on this Thy natal day,
Our tributary anthem pay.

Jesus, to Thee be glory paid,
Blest Offspring of the spotless Maid ;
Thee with thy Sire, His glory's Heir,
And Him, the gracious Comforter.

XXXII

Hymn for Our Lord's Natibity (2.)

A solis ortus cardine

FROM the faint dayspring's eastern goal
   Far as the utmost west,
Come, sing we Christ, the Saviour born
   Of Virgin Mother blest :
The Father of the age to come,
   In servant's form array'd,
That man He might for man atone,
   And ransom whom He made.

Within that Mother's spotless frame
   ·Celestial favour reigns,
A secret load, she ween'd not of,
   The maiden pure sustains :
Her bosom chaste at once becomes
   The temple of her God,

And she, who knew not man, is made
  A heavenly Babe's abode.

He comes, He comes, the Virgin-born
  To Gabriel's promise true ;
He whom, as yet unborn, o'erjoy'd
  The unborn Baptist knew ;
Nor recks He of His bed of hay,
  Nor He the manger heeds ;
Enough the milky breast for Him,
  Who the young ravens feeds.

A shepherd to the shepherds' fold
  The Lord of all is show'd,
Celestial choristers rejoice,
  And angels sing to God.
Now glory, Jesus, be to Thee,
  Whom a pure Virgin bore,
With Father, and with Holy Ghost,
  Henceforth for evermore.

XXXIII

Hymn for the Circumcision

Creator alme siderum

CREATOR of yon circles bright,
  Redeemer, Saviour, Lord of all,
Thy faithful servants' life and light,
  Hear, hear us, Jesus, when we call.

Mankind when Satan captive held
  To save us from his fraudful lure,
Thou camest, by mighty love impell'd,
  A fainting world's support and cure.

When sunk in sin, our common loss,
  Alas ! we knew not to repair,
Thou camest, of woman made, the cross,
  A sinless sacrifice, to bear.

Soon as Thy name is heard to sound,
   Heir of paternal sovereignty,
Celestial potentates uncrown'd
   And fiends infernal bow the knee.

Thee Lord of all our tongues confess,
   Judge of the world when time shall end ;
O with Thy grace Thy servants bless,
   And with Thy sheltering arm defend.

To Him in whom His saints delight,
   His Church on earth, His heavenly host,
Be blessing, honour, glory, might,
   To Father, Son, and Holy Ghost.

XXXIV

Hymn for the Epiphany (1.)

O sola magnarum urbium

FIRST of cities, Bethlehem,
Hail, most favour'd! When He came,
Saviour of the human race,
Thee the Godhead deign'd to grace.

Brighter than the sun's bright car,
And more glorious was the star,
Which in Thee new-born from high
Told the incarnate Deity.

Him what time the Magians saw,
Forth their orient gifts they draw;
Prostrate they with vows unfold
Myrrh, and frankincense, and gold.

Frankincense and gold they bring,
To announce their God and King :
Spice of aromatic myrrh,
To announce His sepulchre.

Jesus, let Thy name be blest,
To the Gentiles manifest ;
To the Father glory be,
With the Spirit, and with Thee !

𝕳𝖞𝖒𝖓 𝖋𝖔𝖗 𝖙𝖍𝖊 𝕰𝖕𝖎𝖕𝖍𝖆𝖓𝖞 (2.)

Crudelis Herodes, Deum

WHY, Herod, why the Godhead fear,
When told Judea's King was near?
Not earthly crowns away to bear
He came, but heavenly to confer.

Led by the star, which ruled their sight,
To seek and find the Lord of Light,
The Magi spread their gifts abroad,
And prostrate own the present God.

The present God the heavens proclaim,
When to the laver pure He came,
The spotless Lamb; and on Him bore
Our sins, who knew not sin before.

78

The God the blushing waters own
By mighty sign, unheard, unknown;
When the pure spring, pour'd forth in wine,
Confest the present power divine.

Now unto Him, the incarnate Son,
Whose glory to the world was shown,
With God the Father glory be,
And, holy Comforter, with Thee!

XXXVI

mn for Christ's Presentation in the Temple

O gloriosa Virginum

ETERNAL Glory of the skies,
Who didst not our low earth despise,
From breasts, by Thee with life endued,
Content to draw Thy milky food :

The Eden, lost by woman's sin,
Thou, made of woman, didst re-win ;
And Mary's holy Son retrieve
The sad incontinence of Eve.

As to Thy Father, throned in heaven,
Thou in His earthly house wast given,
Offering most meet, a holy Child,
By nature sinless, undefiled ;

So to God's house may we repair,
And strive our best to offer there,
With Thee our welcome to secure,
Hearts pure and clean as Thou art pure.

The way, the gate, art Thou alone,
That leads us to the Father's throne;
Thee virgin-born, their life's sole spring,
By Thee redeem'd the nations sing.

Jesus, to Thee be glory paid,
The Son of God, incarnate made :
Thee with Thy Sire, His glory's heir,
And join'd with both the Comforter !

XXXVII

Hymn for Lent (1.)

Ex more docti mystico

Of sacred usage old
   The lenten fast appears;
The Church attends, and calls her fold
   To penitence and tears.

Such rite in days of yore
   The law, the prophets show'd :
Christ to the rite His witness bore,
   And sanctified the mode.

In food, in sport, in sleep,
   'Gainst o'er-indulgence guard ;
And e'en in sinless pleasures keep
   A stricter watch and ward.

F

But chief each act of sin,
　　Each wish, each thought control,
Nor give the tempter place to win
　　Dominion o'er the soul.

Avenging wrath appease,
　　Draw nigh the mercy-seat,
And with meek voice on bended knees
　　The Judge for grace entreat.

'O God, Thy tender love
　　We by our sins offend ;
O pour Thy mercy from above,
　　On us Thy pardon send.

'Think Thou, though weak our frame,
　　Thy workmanship are we :
O give not to another name
　　The honour due to Thee.

'Correct the ill we've done,
  The good we seek improve,
That here and ever we may run
  The way to gain Thy love.

'Thrice Holy One, Thy face
  To us propitious show,
That we Thy servants may the grace
  Of true repentance know.'

XXXVIII

Hymn for Lent (2.)

Audi benigne conditor

HEAR, our all-gracious Father, hear
The prayers which mix'd with many a tear,
Deprest by sense of conscious crime,
We offer in this lenten time.

Kind Searcher of the hearts, alone
To Thee our feeble strength is known :
To Thee we turn : Thy favour show,
And pardon on our sins bestow.

Great are our sins, and numberless :
O spare us, who our sins confess !
Give medicine to the languid soul,
And make us for Thy glory whole.

Grant us to curb the wandering sense,
Subdued by wholesome abstinence ;
That temperate food without, within
May conquer lust and banish sin.

So be Thy will, Thrice Holy, done,
In person Three, in nature One ;
So spring there from our wills subdued
A fruitage holy, just, and good.

XXXIX

Hymn for the Annunciation (1.)

Quem terra, pontus, sidera

HIM whom the skies, the earth, the sea
　　Confess, adore, declare
Lord of that threefold regency,
　　Behold a Virgin bear !

Him whom the light, and time, and space
　　Obey, and own His reign,
Behold, endued with heavenly grace,
　　An earthly Maid contain !

O blest was she, that Virgin bland,
　　Whom He, the Lord of all,
That grasps yon concave in His hand,
　　His mother deign'd to call :

Blest, whom the Angel hail'd, on whom
  The Holy Ghost came down ;
Whose Son, desired their health to come,
  Their health the nations own !

But blest, more blest than she, are they
  By whom His will is done,
Who hear His precepts, and obey
  The Father in the Son.

To Thee, Eternal Son of God,
  Here born of lowly maid,
Is glory in the Godhead owed,
  To Thee be glory paid !

XL

Hymn for the Annunciation (2.)

[ORIGINAL]

Hark ! heard ye not the ancient seer,
　While thus the wondrous promise ran ?
' A Virgin shall conceive, and bear
　A Son, Immanuel—God with man !'

Hark ! hear ye not the Angel bring
　His answering message from the sky ?
' Hail, Virgin blest, from whom shall spring
　A Son, the Son of God most High !'

O Thou, who didst not scorn below,
　The Son of man, with us to dwell,
And us Thy Father's glory show,
　The Son of God, Immanuel ;

Thou, for our sake incarnate made,
 Thy Godhead, lo ! with faith we own,
Or in a servant's form array'd,
 Or partner of Thy Father's throne.

O Jesus, glory be to Thee,
 Return'd to Thy celestial rest,
Throned with Thy Father's majesty,
 In union with the Spirit blest.

XLI

Hymn for Palm Sunday (1.)

Jesu dulcis memoria

SWEET, and with enjoyment fraught,
Is Jesus to the grateful thought :
Far more sweet His presence deem
Than the liquid honey's stream.

By the ear or tuneful tongue
Naught so sweet is heard or sung ;
Naught the heart can muse upon,
Sweet as God's incarnate Son.

Thou, the contrite sinner's stay,
Who Thy goodness can display ?
How to those, who seek Thee, kind !
What, ah what ! to those who find !

Tongue can speak not their delight,
Nor can pen of man indite,
None can know, but they who prove,
What it is their Lord to love !

O be Thou our joy, O Lord!
Thou our future great reward :
And through endless ages be
All our glory but in Thee !

Hymns of glory, notes of praise,
Through eternal ages raise,
To the Father, and the Son,
And the Spirit, Three in One !

XLII

Hymn for Palm Sunday (2.)

Jesu Rex admirabilis

O Jesus, King of Saints adored,
O'er all Thy foes triumphant Lord,
Delightful more than tongue can tell,
Beyond all thought desirable :

If Thou within the heart repair,
Truth shines with noontide lustre there ;
All worldly pomp to vileness turns,
And love with lively ardour burns.

Hail, Saviour ! Thou the heart's delight,
To the dim mind irradiance bright ;
The living fount, whence pleasure flows,
Which the vain world nor seeks nor knows.

Own ye His name ; and seek to prove,
Seek, one and all, the Saviour's love :
With fervour seek ; and, as ye go,
Deep and more deep your fervour grow !

Lord, may my tongue Thy name confess ;
My life Thy holiness express ;
My heart in love of Thee excel,
And ever, ever, with Thee dwell.

O Jesus, whose exalted name
O'er all pre-eminence may claim,
All glory be ascribed to Thee
In the undivided Trinity.

XLIII

Hymn for Good Friday

Lustra sex qui jam peregit, etc.
Pange lingua gloriosi, etc.

SEE the destined day arise !
See, a willing sacrifice,
To redeem our fatal loss,
Jesus hangs upon the cross.

From a tree our loss began
Fatal to primeval man ;
Health attends us from a tree,
God and man, vouchsafed by Thee.

Jesus, who but Thou had borne,
Lifted on that tree of scorn,
Every pang and bitter throe,
Finishing thy life of woe ?

Who but Thou had dared to drain,
Steep'd in gall, the cup of pain ;
And with tender body bear
Thorns, and nails, and piercing spear ?

Thence pour'd forth the water flow'd,
Mingled from Thy side with blood,
Sign to all attesting eyes
Of the finished sacrifice.

Holy Jesus, grant us grace
In that sacrifice to place
All our trust for life renew'd,
Pardon'd sin, and promised good.

Grant us grace to sing to Thee,
In the trinal Unity,
Ever with the sons of light,
Blessing, honour, glory, might.

XLIV

Hymn for Good Friday (2.)

Stabat mater dolorosa

By the cross, sad vigil keeping,
Stood the Mother, doleful, weeping,
  Where her Son extended hung ;
For her soul, of joy bereaved,
Smit with anguish, deeply grieved,
  Lo ! the piercing sword had wrung.

Oh how sad and sore distressed
Now was she, that Mother blessed
  Of the sole begotten One !
Woe-begone, with heart's prostration,
Mother meek, the bitter passion
  Saw she of her glorious Son.

Who on Christ's fond Mother looking,
Such extreme affliction brooking,
  Born of woman, would not weep ?
Who on Christ's fond Mother thinking,
With her Son in sorrow sinking,
  Would not share her sorrow deep

For His people's sins rejected,
She her Jesus, unprotected,
  Saw with thorns, with scourges rent :
Saw her Son from judgment taken,
Her beloved in death forsaken,
  Till His spirit forth He sent.

With Thy Mother's deep devotion,
Make me feel her strong emotion,
  Fount of love, Redeemer kind !
That my heart, fresh ardour proving,
Thee my God and Saviour loving,
  May with Thee acceptance find !

G

XLV

𝔥𝔶𝔪𝔫 𝔣𝔬𝔯 𝔈𝔞𝔰𝔱𝔢𝔯 (1.)

Aurora cœlum purpurat

MORNING spreads her crimson rays,
Heaven resounds with hymns of praise,
Through the earth loud anthems swell,
Heard with rage in vanquish'd hell.

From the dark sepulchral gloom
See the King of Glory come :
See Him now from bondage freed
All His saints to daylight lead.

Vain the tomb securely barr'd,
Sealed stone, and armed guard :
Death is crush'd, and finds his bier
In the Conqueror's sepulchre.

Hence with mourning, hence with tears,
Hence with anxious griefs and fears ;
' Death's subduer is not here,'
Cries His angel minister.

That these thoughts of paschal joy
Ever may our minds employ,
Dead to sin, Thy servants give,
Lord, in holiness to live.

Now be God the Father praised,
With the Son in triumph raised
From the Grave, His Glory's Heir,
And the blessed Comforter.

XLVI

Hymn for Easter (2.)

Ad regias Agni dapes

Now at the Lamb's imperial feast,
In robes of snowy whiteness drest,
The Red Sea pass'd, high songs we sing
Of triumph to the Anointed King.

For us His charity divine
The blood-cup drank of bitter wine :
For us His limbs extended lay,
A sacrifice for love to slay.

With blood the sprinkled door-posts red
The avenging Angel sees with dread :
Apart the startled waves divide,
Pours o'er the foe the refluent tide.

Now Christ our Passover we claim :
The same the sacrifice ; the same,
Pure to the pure of heart and dear,
The unleaven'd bread of truth sincere.

O Thou, true sacrifice from heaven,
To whom the key of hell is given,
By whom the thralls of death unchain'd,
By whom the prize of life regain'd !

Victor of hell's infernal holds,
His trophies Christ revived unfolds ;
And to the heavens' admiring gaze
The captive king of night displays.

That with delight our hearts may burn,
Lord, at Thy paschal feast's return,
Oh, dead to sin, Thy servants give
New born in righteousness to live.

Be the Almighty Father praised;
The Son, who from the dead was raised;
And, the full Godhead to complete,
The Holy Ghost, the Paraclete!

XLVII

Hymn for Easter (3.)

Rex sempiterne cœlitum

THOU, whom their Maker heaven and earth,
  Their King the angels own,
Son, who through boundless ages sharest
  The Almighty Father's throne;
Who Adam, in Thy image made,
  Call'dst forth at nature's birth,
And man became a living soul
  With body form'd of earth:

When Satan's envy and deceit
  Had human-kind defaced,
By Thee was man's primeval form,
  Incarnate Lord, replaced;
Thee, of the Virgin born of old,
  Now new-born from the tomb,

Who bidd'st us buried from the grave
   With Thee reviving come.

Thou, living Shepherd, dost Thy flock
   In bath baptismal lave,
The cleansing laver of our souls,
   And of our sins the grave :
By Thee was borne the cross, the debt
   For our transgressions owed ;
From Thee, the price of our release,
   The blood spontaneous flow'd.

That Thou each year our paschal joy
   Mayst be, Thy servants give,
Regenerate from the death of sin,
   In holiness to live :
So in perpetual hymns shalt Thou,
   Who from the dead wast raised,
The Father, and the Holy Ghost,
   Eternally be praised.

XLVIII

𝕳𝖞𝖒𝖓 𝖋𝖔𝖗 𝖙𝖍𝖊 𝕬𝖘𝖈𝖊𝖓𝖘𝖎𝖔𝖓 (1.)

Æterne Rex altissime

ETERNAL King of heaven on high,
  Hope of Thy Saints beneath,
Crown'd with triumphant majesty,
  The Vanquisher of death :

Thou dost ascend the starry spheres,
  Prompt at the heavenly call,
Which, all unheard by mortal ears,
  Salutes Thee Lord of all :

That of the world, where'er they dwell,
  The tribes may worship Thee ;
And things in heaven, in earth, in hell,
  May bow the subject knee.

Angels behold the change with awe :
　　How sin with flesh began,
And sin by flesh subdued they saw,
　　The Conqueror God in man !

Do Thou from Thy celestial heights
　　Our prize, our pleasure, prove !
The world Thy subject ; Thy delights
　　All worldly joys above.

Thence for our sins the prayer attend,
　　Thy pardoning grace supply,
And down Thy healthful Spirit send
　　To lift our hearts on high.

That when around Thy judgment-seat
　　The skies their radiance pour,
. Thou mayst remit our penal debt,
　　Our forfeit crowns restore.

O Jesus, Glory be to Thee,
  In Thy celestial rest,
Throned with Paternal Majesty,
  And with the Spirit blest!

XLIX

Hymn for the Ascension (2.)

Salutis humanæ Sator

SAVIOUR of men, our joy supreme,
 The heart's desire and pure delight;
Who by Thy love didst those redeem,
 Whom Thou createdst by Thy might:
What unknown love could Thee constrain,
Our sins, all sinless, to sustain?
And the sharp sting of death to try,
That we might live and never die?

Thou break'st through Chaos' old domain,
 Unbind'st the prison'd captive's band,
And with triumphant state dost reign
 In glory on Thy Sire's right hand.

Oh, for our woes benignly feel ;
Our wounds with gentle mercy heal ;
Our eyes, which long Thy face to see,
Glad with the blissful sight of Thee !

Be Thou our heavenward guide and way,
   Thou of our hearts the aim and goal ;
Wipe Thou our tears with joy away,
   Revive and gladden Thou the soul !
To Thee, ascended up to heaven,
Triumphant Son, be glory given ;
And, girt with heaven's adoring host,
Thee, Sire of all ; Thee, Holy Ghost !

L

Hymn for Whit Sunday. (1.)

Veni, Creator Spiritus

COME, Holy Ghost, Creator blest,
Come, visit Thou each willing breast;
And with Thy grace celestial aid
Those whom Thy genial influence made.

O Comforter, Thy grace supply,
Stupendous gift of God most High:
The Fount of life, the Fire of love,
The inward Unction from above.

The gifts of sevenfold grace are thine,
Finger of God, the Father's sign;
The Father's promise, who didst speech
Unknown to lips untutor'd teach.

Lighten our minds with wisdom's beam,
Pour on our hearts affection's stream ;
Our bodies' feeble strength prepare,
With courage, what Thou will'st, to bear.

Far from our home the foe repel :
Make peace within and near us dwell :
Cause that, with Thee to lead and guide,
We turn from evil ways aside.

Confirm our faith, and grant us so
The Father and the Son to know,
That Thee of both we may receive,
And in the triune Name believe.

Be the Eternal Father praised,
From death the Filial Godhead raised ;
And Holy Ghost, Creator, Thou,
Through endless ages even as now.

LI

Hymn for Whit Sunday (2.)

Nunc sancte nobis Spiritus

Thou with the Father and the Son
  United, Spirit blest,
To us Thy healthful grace be shown,
  And foster'd in our breast.
By lips, by mind, by heart exprest,
  May meek confession sound;
May love's bright flame within us rest,
  And spread its warmth around.

Our souls with peace and comfort bless,
  Dissension's heats allay,
And lead us on to righteousness
  By truth's unerring way.
So night by night, and day by day,
  Thy holy will·be done,
While Thee we seek, and with Thee pray
  The Father and the Son.

LII

Hymn for Trinity Sunday (1.)

Summæ Parens Clementiæ

PARENT of all, whose love display'd
Still rules the world Thy bounty made,
Fain would we raise the hymn to Thee,
In substance One, in person Three.

Fain would we chant to Thee the song,
Which through the ages all along
Is chanted by Thy heavenly train,
And earth resounds to heaven again.

Taught by Thy word this festal day
Our homage of true faith we pay :
Oh, in that faith preserve us still,
And shield us evermore from ill :

H

That still our lips Thy praise may show,
And with Thy holy Church below,
Above with Thy angelic host,
Sing Father, Son, and Holy Ghost.

LIII

Hymn for Trinity Sunday (2.)

[ORIGINAL]

HOLY, Holy, Holy, Lord
  God of hosts, essential Good!
God in highest heaven adored,
  Hear our hymn of gratitude.
When in heathen night we lay,
Thou didst o'er us pour Thy ray,
Thee to know, and worship Thee,
In Thy Trinal Unity.

Thou Thy Gospel badest proclaim,
  Thou Thy new-born Church didst lave,
Baptized into Thy threefold name,
  In Thy sanctifying wave :

Thou, from whom the worlds began ;
Thou, redeeming Hope of man ;
Thou, whose hallowing grace is shed
On each chosen faithful head.

O be Thou our strength and stay !
  Save us, we in Thee believe :
By Thee we bless, to Thee we pray,
  And to Thee all glory give.
Holy, Holy, Holy Lord,
Be Thy name in earth adored,
As by Thy celestial host,
Father, Son, and Holy Ghost !

IV

Hymns for Saints' Days

LIV

Hymn on the Holy Angels (1.)

Christe, sanctorum decus Angelorum

CHRIST, of Thy Angel host the grace,
 The Saviour of mankind,
Grant us on high a blessed place
 With that blest host to find.

But first on us below to wait
 Be those blest spirits given,
The court of Thy imperial state,
 The ministry of heaven.

Angel of peace, let Michael come
 From heaven, and hell-ward send
Disastrous war, and here at home
 In one all spirits blend !

Angel of strength, let Gabriel join
   To quell our ancient foes ;
And visit, pleased, each heaven-loved shrine,
   Which erst his trophies rose !

Angel of health, let Raphael speed
   Thy herald from on high,
To guide aright each dubious deed,
   And light each languid eye.

Grant us such aid, Eternal King,
   That we with Thy blest host,
May Thee, Paternal Godhead, sing,
   Thy Son, and Holy Ghost.

LV

Hymn on the Holy Angels (2.)

Te splendor et virtus Patris

THEE, the Father's power and light,
Jesus, Thee, our heart's delight,
Thee, whose lips our life sustain,
Praise we 'mid Thy angel train.

Thousand thousand chiefs at hand
Round Thy throne embattled stand :
Sign of weal to their array,
Michael's hands the cross display.

He, the ancient dragon fell
Smote and drove to nether hell :
He both chief, and rebel crew,
Victor from heaven's rampart threw.

Oh, against that chief of pride
By us be Michael's banner tried ;
And a crown of glory won
From the Lamb's imperial throne.

Glory to the Father be,
Glory, only Son, to Thee,
Glory to the Spirit blest,
Now and evermore addrest.

LVI

Hymn on the Holy Prophets

Quicumque Christum quæritis

Ye who Messiah seek,
　　Aloft your eyes incline,
And see yon ' holy mount ' bespeak,
　　His deathless glory's sign.

There faith may One behold,
　　Majestic, vast, sublime ;
Who ne'er began, ne'er ends ; controll'd
　　By neither space nor time.

'Tis Judah's King, decreed
　　The Gentiles' crown to wear,
The faithful Abraham's promised seed,
　　The royal David's heir.

The Prophets Him record,
   Of Him the signals give ;
The Father witnesses the word,
   And bids us ' hear, believe.'

Jesus, be glory Thine,
   To babes and sucklings known ;
While in the midst Thy symbols shine
   Of heaven's triunal throne.

LVII

Hymn on the Holy Apostles (1.)

Æterna Christi munera

LORD, who didst bless Thy chosen band,
  And forth commission'd send
To spread Thy name from land to land,
  To Thee our hymns ascend.

The princes of Thy Church were they,
  Chiefs unsubdued in fight,
Soldiers on earth of heaven's array,
  The world's unerring light.

Theirs the firm faith of holy birth,
  The hope that looks above,
And, trampling on the powers of earth,
  Their Saviour's perfect love.

In them the Heavens exulting own
  The Father's might reveal'd,
Thy triumph gain'd, begotten Son,
  Thy Spirit's influence seal'd.

Then to Thy Father, and to Thee,
  And to Thy Spirit blest,
All praise for these Thy servants be
  By all Thy Church addrest.

LVIII

Hymn on the Holy Apostles (2.)

Exultet orbis gaudiis

Let the round world with songs rejoice ;
Let heaven return the joyful voice ;
All mindful of the Apostles' fame,
Earth, sky, their Sovereign's praise proclaim !

Thou, at whose word they bore the light
Of gospel truth o'er heathen night,
Oh, still to us that light impart,
To glad our eyes and cheer our heart.

Thou, at whose will to them was given
The key that shuts and opens heaven,
Our chains unbind, our loss repair,
O grant us grace to enter there.

Thou, at whose will they preach'd the word,
Which cured disease, which health conferr'd,
To us its healing power prolong,
The weak support, confirm the strong!

That when Thy Son again shall come,
And speak the world's unerring doom,
He may with them pronounce us blest,
And place us in Thy endless rest.

To Thee, O Father; Son, to Thee;
To Thee, blest Spirit, glory be!
So was it aye for ages past,
So shall through endless ages last.

LIX

𝕳𝖞𝖒𝖓 𝖔𝖓 𝖙𝖍𝖊 𝕳𝖔𝖑𝖞 𝕰𝖛𝖆𝖓𝖌𝖊𝖑𝖎𝖘𝖙𝖘 (1.)

Christi perennes nuntii

PRAISE for Thy Saints to Thee, O Lord,
 Whose heavenly Scriptures, wide unfurl'd
Thy sacred mysteries record,
 And spread them o'er the wondering world.

The darkness far away expell'd,
 The things, which, wrapt in shades of night,
Of old Thy holy seers beheld,
 These now have seen in open light.

Hence, taught by Thee, their records show'd,
 From age to age those records run,
What human things were borne by God,
 By man what things divine were done.

I

Distinct in place, in time remote,
   The selfsame Spirit ruled them all,
Nor fails He, from the rolls they wrote,
   On us with warning voice to call.

And so to God, the One and Three,
   Who calls us from the gloom of night,
His glory's beams reveal'd to see,
   Be praise supreme and sovereign might.

LX

Hymn on the Holy Evangelists (2.)

Sinæ sub alto vertice

FROM thundering skies at Sinai's rock
  Of old the law was given :
And trumpet loud and lightnings spoke
  The present God of heaven.

But now He loves with temper'd might
  A veil of flesh to wear,
And, suited to our feeble sight,
  In milder form appear.

Engraved on stone, the Law defined
  Rules, but no strength convey'd ;
Writ on the heart, the Gospel join'd
  Its rules with power to aid.

This was by voice and faithful pen,
   This by the lives reveal'd,
Answering the voice of sainted men,
   And by their life-blood seal'd.

O Thou, by whose good Spirit taught,
   The words of life they bear,
Plant Thou their records in our thought,
   And ever root them there.

So be, Thrice Holy God, to Thee,
   Whose voice from shades of night
Call'd us Thy glory's beams to see,
   High praise and sovereign might !

LXI

Hymn on the Holy Martyrs (1.)

Sanctorum meritis inclyta gaudia

THE triumphs of the martyr'd saints
  The joyous lay demand,
The heart delights in song to dwell
  On that victorious band :
Those whom the senseless world abhorr'd,
  Who cast the world aside,
Deem'd fruitless, worthless, for the sake
  Of Christ, their Lord and Guide.

For Thee they braved the tyrant's rage,
  The scourge's cruel smart ;
The wild-beast's claw their bodies tore,
  But vanquish'd not the heart :

Like lambs before the sword they fell,
  Nor cry nor plaint exprest ;
For patience kept the conscious mind,
  And arm'd the fearless breast.

What tongue can tell Thy crown prepared
  To wreathe the martyr's head ?
What voice Thy robe of white to clothe
  His limbs with torture red ?
Vouchsafe us, Lord, if such Thy will,
  Clear skies and seasons calm :
If not, the martyr's cross to bear,
  And win the martyr's palm.

LXII

Hymn on the Holy Martyrs (2.)

Invicte Martyr unicum

GREAT God, whose strength Thy martyrs steel'd
    To follow Thy unrivall'd Son,
By whom they braved the battle-field,
    By whom the palm of conquest won :

Thy strength, by sin assail'd, we pray,
    To shield us in our mortal strife,
To drive the taint of guilt away,
    To guard us from the ills of life.

The chains by Thee were loosed, that held
    Thy martyr'd Saints in thrall below :
O be it ours, by Thee upheld,
    Away the world's vile bonds to throw !

O be it ours like them to win
   The vesture white, the branching palm ;
And, free from sorrow as from sin,
   To chant to Thee the holy psalm.

To Thee, above Thy heavenly host,
   O Father, on Thy glory's throne ;
And join'd with Thee, Thy Holy Ghost,
   And, virgin-born, the incarnate Son.

LXIII

𝕳𝖞𝖒𝖓 𝖔𝖓 𝕬𝖑𝖑 𝕾𝖆𝖎𝖓𝖙𝖘 (1.)

Salutis æternæ Dator

O JESUS, source of sanctity,
  In whom Thy servants live,
All glory for Thy Saints to Thee,
  Saviour of men, we give.

All glory for Thy angel train,
  Who heaven's high temple throng;
All glory for those ancient men,
  Bards of prophetic song:

All glory for the messenger,
  Who came Thy face before;
For the blest Maid all glory, her
  Who Thee incarnate bore:

All glory for Thy chosen band,
  To whom the charge was given,
To publish peace from land to land,
  And keep the keys of heaven.

For Thy meek priests, a goodly choir ;
  For them, whose annals boast
Youth, maiden mild, and hoary sire,
  Thy martyrs' noble host.

For these, for all Thy Saints, Thy name
  We laud, and pray that we,
Strong in Thy strength, may follow them,
  As They have follow'd Thee :

But not to them or hymn or prayer
  Present we, due alone
To Thee, and those with Thee who share
  The everlasting throne.

LXIV

Hymn on All Saints (2.)

[ORIGINAL]

For all Thy Saints, O Lord,
 Who strove in Thee to live,
Who follow'd Thee, obey'd, adored,
 Our grateful hymn receive.

For all Thy Saints, O Lord,
 Accept our thankful cry,
Who counted Thee their great reward,
 And strove in Thee to die.

They all in life and death,
 With Thee, their Lord, in view,
Learn'd from Thy Holy Spirit's breath
 To suffer and to do.

Thy mystic members, fit
  To join Thy Saints above,
In one unmix'd communion knit,
  And fellowship of love.

For this Thy name we bless,
  And humbly beg that we
May follow them in holiness,
  And live and die in Thee :

With them the Father, Son,
  And Holy Ghost to praise,
As in the ancient days was done,
  And shall through endless days.

Original Hymns

PRINCIPALLY OF

COMMEMORATION AND THANKSGIVING FOR
CHRIST S HOLY ORDINANCES

LXV

Hymn of Thanksgiving for the One, Holy, Catholic, and Apostolic Church.

WE bless Thee for Thy Church, O Lord,
   Call'd from the world, and seal'd Thine own,
One by the faith of Thy pure word,
   By Thy baptismal laver one.

We bless Thee for Thy Church, ordain'd
   To sanctify the soul from sin,
And cleanse Thine image, erst profaned,
   By holy rite from guilt within.

We bless Thee for Thy Church, which sends
   Thy truth remotest tribes among,
And scatter'd members comprehends
   From every people, kindred, tongue.

We bless Thee for Thy Church, which placed
  Aloft, by signs conspicuous known,
Is on Thine own Apostles based,
  And Jesus Christ the corner-stone.

Lord, for this Church by men design'd
  Thy builders, hallow'd by Thy grace,
One, but to no lone spot confined,
  We bless Thee, and Thy gift embrace.

And pray, that on that sacred site,
  In symbols pure, with guardians true,
Our souls may evermore unite,
  And peace, where Thou ordain'st, ensue.

To Thee, in whom Thy Saints delight,
  Thy Church on earth, Thy heavenly host,
Be blessing, honour, glory, might,
  Thee, Father, Son, and Holy Ghost.

LXVI

Hymn commendatory of Prayer for the Church

O PRAY we for the Church's weal,
    Though earth and hell oppose,
Of good the token and the seal,
    Which God on man bestows.

Pray we, her guides may never cease
    To rule with holy sway;
Her people still in love and peace
    And loyalty obey!

Pray we, that he, who round her lurks
    With craft and subtle wile,
May not, to aid his hostile works,
    The heart of man beguile!

K

Pray we, dissension may in vain
  With unbelief combine,
By open force her towers to gain,
  Or sap with secret mine !

Pray we, that no injurious foe,
  Or rash mistaken friend,
Without may plot her overthrow,
  Within her union rend !

Pray we, that no opprobrious spot,
  Home-bred or brought from far,
The pureness of her faith may blot,
  Her holy worship mar !

O Thou, whose love in man's distress
  Thy Church for refuge gave ;
Do Thou the Church, Thy household, bless,
  And for Thy glory save !

LXVII

Hymn of Thanksgiving for an Apostolical Ministry

ALL praise to Thee, who didst command
  The twelve Thy word to preach,
And willing flocks from every land
  Collect, baptize, and teach.

By them Thy Church's fabric fair
  We hail securely framed,
Thy holy rites establish'd there,
  And there Thy truth proclaim'd.

And still as they to other lands
  By Thee commission'd went,
On other heads they laid their hands,
  And on Thy mission sent.

Transmitted thus from age to age
   In one unbroken line,
Ours is each sacramental pledge
   Of grace and strength divine.

Lord, give us faithful hearts to keep
   Thy own appointed fold,
And with the shepherds of Thy sheep
   Secure communion hold.

To Thee, O Father; Son, to Thee;
   To Thee, O Spirit blest;
All glory in one Godhead be
   By all Thy Saints addrest.

LXVIII

Hymn commemorative of the Ministerial Commission

Who gives the needful power to man,
    Abroad the means of grace to deal,
Release the sinner from his ban,
    His guilt remit, his pardon seal?

He who with consecrated pall
    His chosen Aaron's limbs array'd,
And e'en on Christ with outward call
    The honour of the Priesthood laid.

O dare not then with touch profane,
    That honour on thyself to take;
Nor, oh! pretend with pretext vain,
    A priest unduly call'd to make!

For self-commission'd who may choose
    To seize on God's prerogative,
Heaven's keys without heaven's warrant use,
    Or, what he has received not, give?

Lord, by whose care Thy Church arose
    A goodly frame, Thy Church defend :
And bless her Pastors, sent by those
    Whom Thou hast given the power to send.

To Thee, whom all Thy Saints adore,
    Thy Church on earth, Thy heavenly host,
Be blessing, honour, glory, power,
    Thee, Father, Son, and Holy Ghost.

LXIX

Hymn of Thanksgiving for God's Presence in His Church

Alto ex Olympi vertice

Lo, the Almighty Father's Son
  Quits for earth His heavenly rest,
As a stone descending down
  Sever'd from the mountain's breast.
Of both dwellings He alone
Is the uniting corner-stone.

Ever sounds with holy hymn
  That abode of Saints on high,
Echoing to the Seraphim
  God in Trinal Unity :
Join'd with that, in hymns of praise
We our rival voices raise.

O'er our Temples, Lord of all,
   Thy benignant light extend,
There be present to our call,
   There Thy people's vows attend :
And our fainting souls imbue
Ever with Thy heavenly dew.

There may still the meek request
   Of the faithful heart obtain
Foretaste of those mansions blest,
   And enjoy the precious gain,
Till from bonds corporeal free
We those blessed mansions see.

Now be to the Father done
   Homage, as at all times meet,
To the Father's only Son,
   To the Holy Paraclete ;
Homage such as all things owe,
Saints above, and men below.

LXX

Hymn commemorative of the Pleasure of Social Worship

GLAD is Thy sound, O Sabbath bell,
    Which calls the church-ward road
All who within Thy summons dwell,
    " Come, seek the House of God."

O there 't is joy in one to meet
    Whom one communion blends,
Hold council there in converse sweet,
    And walk therein as friends.

'T is joy to think the angel-train,
    Who 'mid heaven's temple shine,
To seek our earthly temples deign,
    And in our anthems join.

But chief 't is joy to think that He,
  To whom His Church is dear,
Delights her gather'd flock to see,
  Her joint devotions hear.

Then who would choose to walk abroad
  While here such joys are given?
' This is indeed the House of God,
  And this the gate of heaven!'

Who may refuse the proffer'd grace,
  Nor rue with conscious thought,
' Full sure it was the Saviour's place,
  But, ah! I knew it not!'

LXXI

Hymn commemorative of Christ's Presence in Social Worship

How good and pleasant is the sight,
  How great the bliss they share,
When Christ's assembled flock unite
  In his own House of Prayer !
God thither with paternal care
  His face benignant bends ;
And Jesus by His Spirit there
  On faithful hearts descends.

To such, by hallow'd lips exprest,
  His grace confirms His word,
As once Cornelius' house it blest,
  From holy Peter heard :
On prayer and praise in faith preferr'd
  His heavenly dew is shed ;

And He, for all who come prepared,
  Dwells in the mystic bread.

In pure devotion's sacred hours,
  Bound by baptismal sign,
With our companions loved be ours
  In fellowship to join.
And Thou, who bidd'st in rites divine
  Thy Church united meet,
Lord, by Thy presence be it Thine
  Their union to complete !

To God adored in ages past,
  Eternal One in Three,
To God, whose worship aye shall last
  In Trinal Unity ;
To Thee, O Father ; Son, to Thee ;
  To Thee, O Holy Ghost ;
Here in Thy Church all glory be,
  And with Thy heavenly host.

LXXII

Hymn commemorative of God's House of Prayer

THE House of God! What fittest name
May best its noblest use proclaim?
Attend, and hear Himself declare
The House of God, the House of Prayer!

To kneel before Thy mercy's throne ;
To make our wants and wishes known ;
For what our souls, our bodies, need,
Thy love, not our deserts, to plead :

Thy pardon for the past to pray,
Thy bounty for the coming day,
Yet not unmix'd with grateful songs
To Thee, to whom the House belongs !

Such use, O God, befits it best ;
By us be such its use profest :
Nor fail we in our minds to bear,
Thou call'st Thy House the House of Prayer.

O there be present Thou ! Do Thou
Receive the prayer, attend the vow,
Which in Thy house we pay to Thee,
One God in Trinal Unity !

LXXIII

Hymn commendatory of the Reverence due to Holy Places

'PUT off thy shoes, 't is holy ground!'
  A voice to Moses said :
' Nor with unhallow'd things confound
  What God has holy made.'

Whene'er we tread Thy courts, O Lord,
  May no irreverent stain,
In dress or gesture, deed or word,
  Thy sanctuary profane !

Be banish'd thence all mixture base
  Of worldly wish or aim ;
Nor earthly dross defile the place
  Where Thou hast fixt Thy name !

But still may holy hearts be there,
   And holy offerings found ;
And still Thy voice be heard, ' Beware,
   Ye tread on holy ground ! '

To Thee, O Father ; Son, to Thee ;
   To Thee, O Spirit blest ;
All glory in one Godhead be
   By all Thy Church addrest !

LXXIV

Hymn commendatory of the Reverence due to Holy Things

O LORD, whate'er belongs to Thee,
  May we with reverence greet ;
Nor dare Thy holy property
  As things unhallow'd treat !

Thy name no lip with jesting light,
  Or idle speech, profane !
Thy word no ear neglectful slight,
  Or haughtily disdain !

Thy house—may there no reckless foot
  The heedless mind betray !
Nor worldly toils or gauds pollute
  Thy peaceful sacred day !

L

May no vain heart the servants spurn,
   Who Thy commission bear ;
Nor proudly from Thy table turn,
   Nor venture rashly there !

Lord, grant us grace each holy thing
   Occasion meet to make
Of praise for Thee, our heavenly King,
   And prize it for Thy sake !

Thy name, Thy word, Thy house, Thy day,
   Thy priests, and rites divine,
The honour for Thy sake we pay,
   That honour, Lord, is Thine.

Thou seest the duteous heart, when we
   Touch but Thy garment's hem ;
And Thou hast said, 'Who honour me,
   Lo ! I will honour them !'

LXXV

ᚻymn of Thanksgiving for Holy Baptism

GOD of our health, our Life and Light,
That Thou hast purified our sight,
The truth, Thy sacred words express,
To hear, receive, believe, confess ;
Accept the thanks we hymn to Thee,
Lord God Almighty, One and Three !

That, wash'd in Thy thrice Holy Name,
A new relation thence we claim,
And, born by nature sons of earth,
Thence share by grace a heavenly birth ;
Accept the thanks we hymn to Thee,
Lord God Almighty, One and Three !

That thence we worship Thee alone,
And, whom our vows baptismal own,
To Thee the prayer of faith we bring,
To Thee the song of glory sing :
Accept the thanks we hymn to Thee,
Lord God Almighty, One and Three !

That thence the course we're train'd to run
Of goodness at Thy font begun,
Our Saviour's cross to keep in view,
His faith confess, his steps pursue ;
Accept the thanks we hymn to Thee,
Lord God Almighty, One and Three !

O Holy, Holy, Holy, Thou,
God of our health, preserve us now
Firm in Thy worship, fear, and love ;
That we may see Thy face above,
And there our thanks still hymn to Thee.
Lord God Almighty, One and Three !

LXXVI

Hymn commemoratibe of the Church Militant

THE earth it is a battle-field,
　　Where combatants of might
On either side their weapons wield
　　Opposed in mortal fight.

Here lust of flesh, and lust of eye,
　　And pomp and pride of life,
By Satan led, for mastery
　　Maintain unceasing strife.

There soldiers of the incarnate Word
　　In God's proof-armour stand,
Girt with the Spirit's shield and sword,
　　A firm and faithful band.

With her commission'd chiefs to lead,
   The Church that band arrays,
And sign of conquest overhead
   The banner'd Cross displays.

Thus arm'd and marshall'd, in thy sight
   Keep fast that banner'd sign ;
And, Christian, in thy foes' despite
   The triumph shall be thine.

LXXVII

Hymn commemorative of the Church's Instruction of Her Children

Who that hath grace to walk abroad
  In light and liberty divine,
Would leave his children far from God
  In thraldom and in gloom to pine ?

To Thee no such reproofs belong,
  City of God, our Mother dear !
Thy care betimes to train the young,
  Thy Master's will to read and hear :

With heavenly lore enrich the mind ;
  In precepts pure the footsteps lead,
In means, for inward grace design'd,
  In holy prayer and sacred creed.

Then on ! unmoved by hate or scorn,
   By bitter foe, or lukewarm friend ;
Intent the children, thou hast borne,
   Thy babes and sucklings still to tend.

And He who made thee, He who bought,
   And He who hallows thee and thine,
Bless all thy works in duty wrought,
   And make His face on thee to shine !

To Him be praise, in earth and heaven,
   With His redeem'd, His angel host,
By thee and all thy children given,
   To Father, Son, and Holy Ghost !

LXXVIII

Hymn commendatory of Family Worship

O 'T IS a scene the heart to move,
   When households day by day,
Whom God unites in social lovè,
   Unite His grace to pray !

What though the number be but small,
   Whenever two or three
Join on the Saviour's name to call,
   There in the midst is He.

When faithful and repentant hearts
   His heavenly grace ensue,
His grace entreated He imparts
   To many or to few.

O come then, and with joint accord
   In household worship meet;
And mindful of the Saviour's word,
   The Saviour's boon entreat!

To Him, and those with Him who dwell
   In fellowship entire,
O let our tongues our wishes tell,
   O let our hearts aspire!

To Him, with God the Father join'd,
   And God the Spirit blest,
By all in social bands combined
   Be glory joint addrest.

LXXIX

Hymn of Thanksgiving for the Church's Scriptural Worship

LORD, not to us, we claim it not,
  To Thee be all the praise,
That no profane inveterate spot
  Our mother Church o'erlays ;
That, as in her primeval days,
  From intermediate stain
Cleansed by Thy word, to Thee she pays
  Unsullied rites again.

To no material form confined,
  A spirit pure alone,
We serve Thee not in likeness shrined
  Of bread, or wood, or stone :
Nor saint nor angel at Thy throne
  We crave to intercede,

With Thee for our misdeeds atone,
  With Thee for mercy plead.

But far remote we seek Thy face,
  Hid in Thy heavenly seat ;
And, sole transmitter of Thy grace,
  The Saviour's name entreat :
And thus to Thee with honour meet
  We hymn the grateful lay,
Whose word recall'd our erring feet,
  And warn'd us how to pray.

To Thee, adored in ages past,
  Eternal One and Three,
To Thee, whose worship aye shall last,
  In trinal Unity :
To Thee, O Father ; Son, to Thee ;
  And Thee, O Spirit blest ;
By Saints on earth all glory be
  With Saints in heaven addrest !

LXXX

Hymn of Thanksgiving for the Church's Liturgy

O LORD, with ever-varying phrase
   We kneel not at Thy throne ;
More fain the Church her homage pays
   In language tried and known.

Such worship to Thy name of old
   Thy chosen people brought ;
Such worship to His infant fold
   The incarnate Saviour taught.

Such worship, as her cords she spread,
   The growing Church instill'd ;
By Thy own heaven-taught Pastors fed,
   And with Thy Spirit fill'd.

Still by the self-same Spirit train'd
  In her reviving day,
We bless Thee that Thy Church retain'd
  Thy worship's ancient way :

That still she loves Thy grace to seek
  In language still the same,
Most meet her own desires to speak,
  Most worthy of Thy name.

To Thee, O Father; Son, to Thee ;
  To Thee, O Spirit blest ;
All glory in one Godhead be
  By all Thy Church addrest !

LXXXI

Hymn of Thanksgiving for the Church's Primitive Character

WHEN first divine Religion blest
The islands of our distant West,
From lips apostolic she bore
The truth to our benighted shore :

The temples of our heathen waste
With rites apostolic she graced :
And from Apostles' hands convey'd
The Mitre to the hallow'd head.

Blest be our gracious God, that we,
From dreams of man's invention free,
Still in His own Apostles' fold,
Their creed, their rites, their orders hold :

The truth, proclaim'd by them, believe ;
The rites, by them consign'd, receive ;
And welcome what God's word commands,
From duly consecrated hands.

By self-form'd ways, who will, may go :
Enough for us, O God, to know,
Thy Church how Thy first stewards led ;
And in those ancient pathways tread.

Praise God, adored in ages past ;
Praise God, whose praise shall ever last ;
His Church on earth, His heavenly host,
Praise Father, Son, and Holy Ghost.

LXXXII

Hymn commendatory of taking part in Worship

O COME, and let the assembly all
  To serve our God unite ;
And, mindful of the social call,
  Partake the social rite !

In token of the common vow,
  Be ours with one consent
The worship of the lowly brow,
  And knees devoutly bent !

Be ours the worship of the tongue,
  In self-same sounds agreed,
The meek confession, holy song,
  Pure prayer, and faithful creed !

M

But chief inflamed with heavenly fire,
    Devotion's better part,
Be ours, instinct with one desire,
    The worship of the heart!

Let each, let all, their prayers above
    In one oblation blend:
And God, the God of peace and love,
    On all, on each, descend!

To Thee, O Father; Son, to Thee;
    To Thee, O Spirit blest:
All glory in one Godhead be
    By all Thy Saints addrest!

LXXXIII

Hymn commemorative of the Object of Christian Worship

ARISE, your voices all unite,
 And lift your hearts above,
To God, the Lord of power and might,
 To God, whose name is Love.

To Him, who us, and earth, and skies,
 With all their armies made,
From us, from all, let anthems rise,
 To God the Father paid.

To Him, for us and all mankind
 Whose death redemption won,
By us, by all, be hymnings join'd
 Of praise to God the Son.

To Him, who us and all His fold
　　With sanctity arrays,
To God, from all, His saints enroll'd,
　　The Holy Ghost be praise.

To God, whose name His word reveals,
　　Whom all His saints confess,
Whose grace His faithful promise seals
　　To save, to cleanse, and bless ;

To God, from whom all blessings flow
　　Eternal One in Three,
From all His saints above, below,
　　Eternal glory be !

LXXXIV

Hymn commendatory of Christian Fellowship

FATHER of all, from whom we trace
  Our universal kind,
Teach us to all of human race
  To show a brother's mind.

Saviour of men, 't was Thine the pain
  Of death for all to bear,
In concord all Thy followers train,
  Meet for the name they share.

Spirit of grace, God's chosen fold
  Who lavest with heavenly dew,
O grant that all, the truth that hold,
  May peace with all ensue.

O might mankind in love agree,
  Sons of one parent stock !
But chief may Christian verity
  Connect the Christian flock !

May truth to all, that hear its sound,
  A bond of union prove ;
And fellowship of faith be crown'd
  With fellowship of love !

Paternal Godhead, praise to Thee,
  Thy Spirit, and Thy Son !
And keep Thy Church in unity,
  As Thou with them art one !

LXXXV

Hymn commemoratibe of Prayer in, and to Christ

HOLY JESUS, in whose name
Thou hast bid Thy servants claim
Of the Father's love, to grant
All the good they wish or want :
Trusting in Thy name alone,
Draw we near Thy Father's throne.

Holy Jesus, at whose name,
Through this universal frame,
By the Almighty Sire's decree
All its dwellers bow the knee :
To Thy Father's name we join
In co-equal worship Thine.

Son of man, to whom is given,
With the Majesty of heaven,
Partner Thou of man's estate,
For mankind to mediate :
Hear us, when to Thee we plead
For Thy flock to intercede !

Son of God, to whom of right,
Partner of Thy Father's might,
' Sole, adorable, and true,'
Empire o'er the world is due :
Hear us, when on Thee we call
For Thy blessing, Lord of all !

Saviour of the world, to Thee
Ever bows the Church her knee ;
Thee, her only Advocate ;
Thee, exalted to Thy state,
With the Holy Ghost most high
In the Father's majesty.

LXXXVI

Hymn commendatory of the Church's Signs of Reverence

In bath baptismal who can know
 By Christ repair'd our primal loss,
Yet grudge the new-born Christian's brow,
 Sign of His faith, the Saviour's Cross ?

Who at Christ's mystic board can feel
 The value of His heavenly food,
Yet grudge in lowly guise to kneel,
 In memory of the Saviour's Blood ?

Who can in thought to heaven ascend,
 Whence man the Son of God became,
Yet grudge the head, the knee, to bend,
 In honour of the Saviour's Name ?

Such honour deem we justly Thine ;
  Such honour, Lord, wilt Thou approve :
Nor slight in each expressive sign
  Thy Church's reverence, faith, and love.

Lord, to Thy name for ever be
  From us, as from Thy heavenly host,
All glory paid ; and one with Thee,
  The Father, and the Holy Ghost.

LXXXVII

Hymn commemorative of the Confession of Sins

BEFORE Thy mercy's throne
   Thy succour, Lord, we seek,
For Thou art good and great alone,
   All helpless we and weak.

Like sheep, that go astray,
   Our wilful course we've run,
From what Thou wouldst, have turn'd away,
   And what Thou wouldst not, done.

To us belong dismay
   Of heart and shame of face :
To Thee our sorrows to allay,
   Our guiltiness efface.

To us confession meek,
  The penitential prayer :
To Thee the words of peace to speak,
  The contrite heart to spare.

O spare our sins confest,
  The penitents restore :
On them, who turn to Thee for rest,
  Thy healthful Spirit pour !

Pour, for the Saviour's sake,
  Thy blessing's heavenly dew,
On those who fain would sin forsake,
  And Thy pure ways pursue.

While at Thy mercy's throne
  In His prevailing name,
Who died for sinners to atone,
  Thy promised grace we claim.

LXXXVIII

Hymn of Thanksgiving for the Remission of Sins

GOD of our health, all praise to Thee,
  Whose goodness to Thy Church has given,
Wrought by Thy Son, the golden key,
  That opes the eternal gates of heaven.

When hallow'd lips, by Thee ordain'd,
  Pronounce Thy mercy's pardoning seal,
Repentant hearts, which faith hath train'd,
  A peace, the world can give not, feel.

But to the sinner's reckless ear
  No joy those sounds of love impart :
The undiscerning mind they sear,
  The worldly soul, the harden'd heart.

God of our health, whose word empowers
   Thy Church offences to remit,
Thy pardon, lo, we crave !   Be ours
   In faith our former sins to quit :

So on our hearts may pardon light,
   Our lives be holy, pure, and good ;
Strong in Thy Spirit's quickening might,
   Cleansed by a sinless Saviour's blood !

LXXXIX

Hymn commendatory of our Daily Prayers

As kneeling at Thy mercy's throne
  Our daily prayers we lay,
With hearts sincere, and humble tone ;
  Lord, hear us when we pray.

When from whate'er may hurt or harm
  We Thy deliverance crave ;
Hear Thou, and stretch Thy gracious arm,
  And us from evil save.

When what supply our wants demand,
  Of Thee our tongues require ;
Hear Thou, and ope Thy bounteous hand,
  And grant the meek desire.

When for our kind's or country's wealth
   We plead, for friend or foe ;
Hear Thou, and what may tend to health
   Of each, on each bestow.

Hear, Lord, the vows Thy servants make,
   Naught can their merits claim :
'T is all for Thy great mercies' sake,
   And in their Saviour's name.

xc

Hymn commemorative of Singing Praises to God

PRAISE we our God! our voices raise
The Lord of hosts, our God, to praise!
To Him, by whom our lips unclose,
The mouth her richest homage owes.

Who, 'mid glad anthems pealing high,
Would wait in lifeless silence by?
When worship claims the posture fit,
Who in irreverent ease would sit?

Rise, rise, and act the angels' part,
In gesture, voice, and holy heart;
Who loud their Hallelujahs sing,
With crowns cast off, and folded wing.

N

194

O may we here our homage pay,
Like angels in the realms of day ;
That we in future worlds may hymn
God's praises with the Cherubim.

Praise Him, adored in ages past ;
Praise Him, whose praise shall ever last :
Praise him amid his heavenly host ;
Praise Father, Son, and Holy Ghost.

XCI

Ḥymn commemorative of Thanksgibing to God

WHAT can the heart more pleasant feel,
　What more befits the generous thought,
Than the warm glow of grateful zeal,
　For acts of love undue, unsought ?

What sounds, the sense or soul to move,
　More tuneable can tongue express,
Than, mindful of such acts of love,
　The strains of holy thankfulness ?

Lord, as with wondering eyes we scan
　Of all Thy love the countless sum ;
But most the ransom paid for man,
　The present grace, the bliss to come :

O prompt us Thou, the sovereign Good,
   Thy undeserved, unask'd for, care
To feel with lively gratitude,
   And with our thankful lips declare.

And ne'er, oh ! ne'er may we forget
   Deep in our inmost hearts to lay ;
And, as we can, the mighty debt
   With pure and holy lives to pay !

To Father, Son, and Holy Ghost,
   For all His mercy's boundless store,
For His redeeming love the most,
   Be glory now and evermore.

XCII

Hymn of Thanksgiving for the Holy Scriptures

ACCEPT, O Lord, thy servants' thanks
  For Thy enlivening word,
By Thy most Holy Spirit taught,
  By holy Prophets heard :
That word in Thy recording book
  From age to age descends,
Her teaching here Thy Church begins,
  And here her teaching ends.

Whate'er of truth the soul can need
  To clear her darkling sight,
Whate'er to check the wandering feet
  And guide their course aright ;

Whate'er of fear the bad to daunt,
  Of hope the good to cheer ;
All that may profit man, O Lord,
  Thy bounty gives us here.

Join'd with our household's little church,
  And in our lonely hours,
And in the assembly of the Saints,
  That sacred word be ours,
To read and hear, to mark and learn,
  And inwardly digest ;
And He, who gave the word, may He
  On those who learn it rest !

Thence on our hearts may lively faith
  Celestial comfort pour,
With patience, lightener of our ills,
  And hope that looks before :

That we, with Thy united Church,
  May lift our souls above,
And with one mind and mouth proclaim
  Thy glory, God of love !

XCIII

Hymn of Thanksgiving for the Church's Creeds

Of frail and fluctuating mind
  Is man, and apt to stray ;
And baseless objects, ill defined,
  His sight and steps betray.

And though Thy word, O God, be true,
  And beam with heavenly light,
Of those it oft deceives the view,
  Who scan it not aright.

We deem it then Thy act of grace
  And providential care,
That not alone we're left to trace
  Thy truths unfolded there :

Which widely scattered o'er Thy roll,
　　And thence in one combined,
Thy Church presents, unmix'd and whole,
　　Arranged, secured, defined.

Hence raised she in her ancient days
　　The symbols of her creed,
To guard her sons from error's maze,
　　Their feet aright to lead.

And we those forms of wholesome words
　　Maintain from days of old ;
And what the Church her faith records,
　　We still unshaken hold.

Then glory to our gracious God,
　　The Three in One, be paid,
As ever by His Church avow'd,
　　And by His word display'd.

•

XCIV

𝕳𝖞𝖒𝖓 𝖔𝖋 𝕿𝖍𝖆𝖓𝖐𝖘𝖌𝖎𝖇𝖎𝖓𝖌 𝖋𝖔𝖗 𝖙𝖍𝖊 𝕻𝖚𝖗𝖊 𝕱𝖆𝖎𝖙𝖍

THAT Thou Thy servants hast not placed,
　　To roam by reason's glimmering ray
Through nature's unenlighten'd waste,
　　Thee, God of love, our thanks we pay !

That Thou with Thy celestial lore
　　Illumin'st our benighted sight,
To know, confess Thee, and adore,
　　Our thanks we pay Thee, God of light !

To find Thee, passes reason's reach :
　　But taught Thy Godhead to discern
Reveal'd, what Thou hast deign'd to teach,
　　She prompts the humble heart to learn.

O may no love of worldly joys,
    Or worldly cares, Thy truth neglect ;
Nor human wisdom's specious toys,
    Nor pride of human power reject !

For Thou hast said, and we receive
    Thy word as law, Thy will as fate,
Who will Thy Gospel not believe,
    On him Thy penal doom shall wait.

God, in whose name by mystic sign
    Baptized Thy saints Thy faith confess,
To keep us in Thy faith be Thine,
    Be ours Thy triune name to bless !

To Thee, whom all Thy saints adore,
    Thy Church below, Thy heavenly host,
Be blessing, honour, glory, power,
    Thee, Father, Son, and Holy Ghost !

XCV

Hymn commendatory of Faith and Good Works

In God's own garden stands a tree,
    Fast fix'd in earth its root,
Bathed in heav'n's dews, and fair to see,
    And charged with goodly fruit.

Like that fair tree's no fruitage grows,
    So pleasant and so good :
What else a specious semblance shows,
    Affords no wholesome food.

But should that tree unfruitful wax
    Of good, like thorn or brier,
'T is doom'd to feel the hewer's axe,
    And feed the vengeful fire.

The tree that God's own garden breeds,
   Faith is that goodly tree :
The fruits, it genders, are the deeds
   Of Christian charity.

God, may Thy Church, that cultured field
   Which Thou hast fenced around,
Such trees in rich profusion yield,
   With such good fruit abound.

For deeds, though fair, Thou wilt not own,
   Save of Thy Spirit bred ;
And faith, unfruitful and alone,
   By Thee is counted dead.

XCVI

𝕳𝖞𝖒𝖓 𝖔𝖋 𝕿𝖍𝖆𝖓𝖐𝖘𝖌𝖎𝖛𝖎𝖓𝖌 𝖋𝖔𝖗 𝕾𝖕𝖎𝖗𝖎𝖙𝖚𝖆𝖑 𝕴𝖓𝖘𝖙𝖗𝖚𝖈𝖙𝖔𝖗𝖘

WE thank Thee for the truths, O Lord,
Which Thy unerring rolls record ;
Nor less we thank Thee for the aid,
By Thine appointed guides convey'd.

Apt are those rolls the steps to lead,
That ofttimes he who runs may read ;
Yet oft awaits a harder part,
The mind unlearn'd, the unstable heart.

Not vain the tale, by Thee enroll'd,
Of that illustrious student told,
By Philip's sapient teaching won
To see and own Thy promised Son.

Nor vain Thy warning of the minds,
Blown here and there by wavering winds,
Which read Thy word, alas! unblest,
And to their own destruction wrest.

Then thanks to Thee, whose care provides
Thy Church's help, our priestly guides;
Light from their urns that we may draw,
And read undimm'd Thy perfect law.

To Thee, O Father; Son, to Thee;
To Thee, blest Spirit, glory be;
For all the good Thy creatures prove,
But most for Thy redeeming love.

𝕳ymn commemoratibe of 𝕳earing 𝕲od's 𝕸inisters

OFT as in God's own house we sit,
  And hear the Preacher there,
Precursive to the grave discourse,
  The holy text declare ;
Bethink we well, whose name he bears,
  And whence his word is given,
The steward of God's mysteries,
  The minister of heaven.

Away then with the itching ear,
  That craves the pleasant tongue ;
Away the eyes that for the sight
  Of art theatric long ;

Away for simple phrase sincere
    The judgment too refined ;   1
But most away the o'erweening heart
    And self-sufficient mind.

Be rather ours to bear our part
    With awe and godly fear ;
O'erlook the frailties of the man,
    And God's high message hear :
Be from our hearts, howe'er disguised,
    The pride of life exiled ;
And heaven's best gift ingraft instead,
    The meekness of a child.

O God, to Thy ambassador
    Thus speaking in Thy name,
Aid us to show the deep respect
    Thy messenger may claim ;

To listen, ponder, and digest
Each truth and law divine,
And prize Him for His office sake,
And, Lord of all, for Thine!

XCVIII

Hymn of Thanksgiving for the Holy Communion

Thy house each day of hallow'd rest
  With joyful heart, O Lord, I tread ;
Most joyful, for the holy feast
  When Thy mysterious board is spread.

When in Thy house Thy servants meet,
  There always in the midst art Thou :
To offer at the mercy seat
  The humble heart, the fervent vow.

But most, when holy hands dispense,
  Ordain'd by Thee, salvation's sign,
Thy presence glads the inward sense,
  Thy Spirit, and Thy grace divine ; '

Sweet peace and comfort to impart,
   Beyond this lower world's control ;
To cleanse and sanctify the heart,
   To strengthen and refresh the soul.

O ever there, a willing guest,
   May I, and not unworthy be :
And there, with Thy communion blest,
   My Lord and Saviour, dwell with Thee !

For all Thy bounty to mankind,
   For Thy redeeming love the most,
All praise to Thee, and with Thee join'd,
   The Father and the Holy Ghost !

XCIX

Hymn commendatory of the Holy Communion

No ! when He bids me seek His face,
 Away I will not turn :
Nor His appointed means of grace
 With proud self-wisdom spurn.
The pathway to remember Him,
 Which He vouchsafes to show,
I will not leave, and lightly deem,
 That I may blameless go.

True : I'm a sinner : but His blood
 For sinners once was shed :
For sinners now this heavenly food,
 His mystic feast, is spread.

For sinners, who their sins would quit,
　And to His succour fly,
Their past offences to remit,
　And future strength supply.

Forgive me, Lord ! my heart incline
　To run the Christian race,
And first beneath Thy stated sign
　To seek Thy promised grace :
Thy grace with thankful heart to seek,
　With faith that soars above,
Repentance true, obedience meek,
　And universal love.

Though much unworthy, Lord, of Thee,
　Yet no presumptuous guest,
May these my wedding-garment be,
　To deck me for Thy feast !

The willing heart wilt Thou receive,
  Who didst for sin atone ;
And not for our deserts forgive,
  But, Saviour, for Thine own.

C

Hymn commemoratibe of the 'Thrice Holy'

BRIGHT the vision that delighted
 Once the sight of Judah's seer,
Sweet the countless tongues united
 To entrance the Prophet's ear.
Round the Lord in glory seated,
 Cherubim and Seraphim
Fill'd His temple, and repeated
 Each to each th' alternate hymn.

' Lord, Thy glory fills the heaven,
 Earth is with its fulness stored ;
Unto Thee be glory given,
 Holy, Holy, Holy Lord ! '

Heaven is still with glory ringing,
 Earth takes up the angels' cry,
' Holy, Holy, Holy,' singing,
 'Lord of Hosts, the Lord most high !'

Ever thus in God's high praises,
 Brethren, let our tongues unite ;
Chief the heart when duty raises
 God-ward at His mystic rite :
With His Seraph train before Him,
 With His holy Church below,
Thus conspire we to adore Him,
 Bid we thus our anthem flow !

' Lord, Thy glory fills the heaven,
 Earth is with its fulness stored ;
Unto Thee be glory given,
 Holy, Holy, Holy Lord !

Thus Thy glorious name confessing,
  We adopt Thy angels' cry,
Holy, Holy, Holy ! blessing
  Thee the Lord of Hosts most high !'

CI

Hymn commemorative of the Day of Holy Rest

BLEST day, by God in mercy given,
  To soothe, refresh, and cheer,
We greet thee best of all the seven,
  And hold thee doubly dear.

We prize thee as the day of rest,
  Which toil nor travail knows ;
The Sabbath Day, when man and beast
  From week-day works repose.

We prize thee as the day design'd
  From worldly studies freed,
The holy Day, to train the mind
  To holy thought and deed.

We prize Thee as God's living sign,
　Join'd with His faithful word,
How man was form'd by power divine,
　By power divine restored.

Blest day, by God's commandment made
　The goodliest of the seven,
Type of the heavenly rest, our aid
　In journeying to heaven :

May holy thoughts and holy rites
　Thy peaceful hours employ,
Till we through love of such delights
　God's endless rest enjoy !

There hymn, amid His heavenly host,
　The praise on earth begun,
Of Father, Son, and Holy Ghost,
　The Uncreated One !

CII

Hymn of Thanksgiving for the Day of Holy Rest

O COME, and for His day of rest
Praise Him, who hallowed it and blest,
And gave the law, when time began,
Memorial of His works to man.

Praise Him, who to the chosen seed
Confirm'd the law at first decreed ;
And 'mid His statutes, graved on stone,
Renew'd, and made His Sabbath known.

Praise Him who to His twelve consign'd,
And will'd His Church to bear in mind,
The day, her buried Saviour rose,
Her day for sanctified repose.

Praise Him, that, still with sacred awe,
His Church maintains His primal law ;
And keeps for man, from death released,
Redemption's with creation's feast.

To keep this primal law of Thine,
In mercy, Lord, our hearts incline :
To us Thy holy day be blest,
And lead us to Thy heavenly rest !

CIII

Hymn commemoratibe of the Church's Greater Festibals

SAVIOUR of men, our hope and rest,
　　As round the yearly seasons run,
Train'd by Thy Church, each solemn feast
　　We hail Thee, God's incarnate Son !

Week after week Thy Advent told,
　　At length we hail Thee Virgin-born,
While Angels to the Shepherds' fold
　　Announce with chants redemption's morn.

When, guided by the new-formed star,
　　Their gifts the eastern sages bring,
In Thee, the Gentiles' light from far,
　　We hail Judea's promised King.

We hail Thee, to the temple brought,
    The temple's Glory and its Lord :
Thy conflict in the desert fought,
    We hail Thee King o'er fiends abhorr'd.

Dark scenes of sorrow come : and lo !
    In Salem's courts, in Kedron's vale,
On that sad hill of shame and woe,
    Thee sufferer for our sins we hail.

Loosed from the tomb that held Thee dead,
    Ascended to Thy seat on high,
And thence Thy Holy Spirit shed,
    We hail Thee crown'd with majesty.

All hail, our Saviour ! as we store
    Thy acts in mind each solemn feast,
Still more we love Thee, and adore
    In Thee the Father's form exprest.

CIV

Hymn commemorative of 'The Way, the Truth, and the Life'

HOLY Jesus, Saviour blest,
As by passion strong possest,
Through this world of sin we stray,
Thou to guide us art 'the Way.'

Holy Jesus, when the night
Of error blinds our clouded sight,
Round the cheering day to throw,
Saviour, then 'the Truth' art Thou.

Holy Jesus, when our power
Fails us in temptation's hour,
All unequal to the strife,
Thou to aid us art 'the Life.'

P.

Who would reach His heavenly home,
Who would to the Father come,
Who the Father's presence see,
Jesus, he must come by Thee.

Channel of the Father's grace,
Image of the Father's face,
Saviour blest, incarnate Son,
With the Father Thou art one.

Glory to the Father be,
Glory, only Son, to Thee ;
And, of equal power confest,
Glory to the Spirit blest.

CV

Hymn to the Comforter for 'Faith, Hope, and Charity'

'COME, Holy Ghost, my soul inspire!'
Spirit of the Almighty Sire,
Spirit of the Son Divine,
Comforter, Thy gifts be mine!

Holy Spirit, in my breast
Grant that lively 'faith' may rest,
And subdue each rebel thought
To believe what Thou hast taught!

When around my sinking soul
Gathering waves of sorrow roll,
Spirit blest, the tempest still,
And with 'hope' my bosom fill!

Holy Spirit, from my mind
Thought, and wish, and will unkind,
Deed and word unkind remove,
And my bosom fill with 'love !'

Faith, and hope, and charity,
Comforter, descend from Thee,
' Thou th' anointing Spirit art,'
These Thy gifts to us impart ;

Till our faith be lost in sight,
Hope be swallow'd in delight,
And love return to dwell with Thee
In the threefold Deity !

CVI

Hymn commendatory of the Church's Minor Festivals

WHAT more befits the Church's name,
Than to uphold the saintly fame
Of those, who in the Saviour's might
Fought for His sake the Christian fight?

What more befits the Church's care,
Than to provoke her sons to share
In rival deeds and rival praise,
By monuments of festal days?

Through perils they, and toil, and strife,
Held fast ' the way, the truth, the life ;'
Weigh'd heavenly gain with earthly loss,
And chose and bore the Saviour's cross.

Led by Thy Church be ours, O God,
To tread the path Thy servants trod ;
Ourselves with Thine elect acquaint,
And love the Master in the Saint !

All blessing, honour, glory, power,
To Thee, whom all Thy saints adore,
Thy Church on earth, Thy heavenly host ;
Thee, Father, Son, and Holy Ghost.

CVII

Hymn of Thanksgiving for the First Preachers of the Gospel

For those, who first proclaim'd Thy word,
Accept Thy Church's thanks, O Lord!
For Andrew's prompt obedience, free
From worldly lures, in following Thee;
For Thomas' noble creed avow'd
In owning Thee his Lord and God;
For the bright beams of light which shone
From him, Thy own belovèd John.

For martyr'd Stephen's meek appeal;
Repentant Paul's well-temper'd zeal;
For him, the Pastor true, whose call
Supplied the faithless traitor's fall;

And him, thrice charged to feed Thy flock,
Whose faith is aye Thy Church's rock;
And him, of Thy commission'd band
The first to feel the murderous brand!

For him, that faithful man and good,
With Thy blest Spirit's gifts endued;
For them, through all Thy Churches known,
Whose praise is in the gospel shown:
For these, for all, who spread Thy word,
Accept Thy Church's thanks, O Lord;
And grant that she like sons may bear,
Meet for Thy work, and worthy her!

CVIII

Hymn of Thanksgiving for the Church's Reformers

WHILE for Thy Saints, who pour'd abroad
   Thy gospel's glorious light
Through heathen lands, we bless, O God,
   Thy wisdom, love, and might ;
We fain would their loved names unite,
   Who pierced the clouds obscure,
Which hid from our forefathers' sight
   That gospel's radiance pure.

To clear Thy truth their heart's desire,
   Their life's pursuit and aim,
They mark'd unmoved the martyr's pyre,
   Unmoved they felt the flame :

There lit, the fire a sign became
   Through all the land to prove,
How they could bear Thy cross and shame,
   Who for Thy glory strove.

Hence in Thy truth Thy Church delights,
   From old corruptions freed;
Unblemish'd worship, spotless rites,
   And unadulterate creed:
Hence Thy pure words her children lead
   To speak the united prayer,
Their Saviour's name alone to plead,
   His cup of blessing share.

O God, whose love our country's guides
   Once nerved with courage strong,
And still o'er us their sons presides,
   Accept our grateful song.

And oh ! the truth, revived among
　　Our sires from times of old,
Do Thou to future times prolong,
　　And grant our sons to hold !

CIX

Hymn of Thanksgiving for the Church's Moderation

WE deem and own it, Lord, a proof
　Of Thy peculiar grace,
That from intemperate zeal aloof,
　With calm, considerate pace,
Our Mother Church aye runs her race,
　Unsway'd by fancies new,
And in Thy vineyard holds her place,
　A fruitful branch and true.

'T is of Thy grace, that long beguiled
　From Thy straight path to stray,
She scann'd Thy volume undefiled
　For truth's unerring way :

Nor fail'd to note, for truth's essay,
  How, in her days of yore,
Thy universal Church the sway
  Through scatter'd nations bore.

'T is of Thy grace that thus we hold
  Sound forms of faith divine ;
That thus Thy shepherds rule Thy fold
  In one unbroken line ;
That thus each sacramental sign
  Thy flock together binds ;
And thus our common voices join
  To speak consentient minds.

Blest, who, by Thy enlivening grace,
  With meek obedience run
And faith unfeign'd their Christian race,
  As by the Church was done,

When, by Thy chosen twelve begun,
　She first Thy blessing sought,
Establish'd by Thy only Son,
　And by Thy Spirit taught.

CX

Hymn commendatory of Church Union

BLEST with unearthly bliss were they,
Who saw the Church's infant day,
And strove their Christian part to bear,
By birth baptismal join'd with her.

The truth, which Christ's Apostles taught,
Then ruled each faithful convert's thought;
Each aim'd in unity to keep
Unrent the Apostles' fellowship :

The bread, with rites harmonious broke,
The union of all hearts bespoke ;
And prayer, with lips united pray'd,
The union of all minds display'd.

O thus that Christians still would live,
And thus delightful witness give,
How well the debt of love they know,
To Christ and to His Church they owe !

Lord, train us still on earth to join
Thy holy Church in acts divine !
Till we a closer union prove,
Join'd to Thy unseen Church above.

There all at once Thy first-born sing
Joint Hymns to Thee, Eternal King ;
And with one voice Thy angel host
Praise Father, Son, and Holy Ghost.

CXI

Hymn condemnatory of Schism

A SIN there was in ancient days,
   The Apostle names its name,
And marks its nature with dispraise,
   The Church's bane and shame.
Who form'd without her factions new,
   Or nourish'd feuds within,
Or scorn upon her rulers threw,
   Were guilty of that sin.

Observant of the Apostle's word,
   The Church its guilt discerns,
Against it prays her gracious Lord,
   And for deliverance yearns.

Q

Nor falsehood, for celestial truth,
  By her accuser spread,
Nor heresy's envenom'd tooth,
  Awakes a livelier dread.

Alas, that we with little care
  Her supplications heed ;
But, though our lips pronounce the prayer,
  Too oft commit the deed :
Too oft against Thee, God of love,
  And Thy command offend ;
And to Thy name our right disprove,
  While we Thy body rend.

O might we all, Thy name who bear,
  Beneath one sovereign Head
One body own, one faith declare,
  Partake one mystic bread ;

By all might one pure worship be.
  To Thee, One God, addrest;
To Thee, O Father; Son, to Thee;
  And Thee, O Spirit blest.

CXII

Hymn commemorative of the Punishment of Schism

WHAT means that loud portentous cry
    Of terror strange from yonder tent?
From Korah, and his company,
    That strange portentous cry is sent.
A Levite, priestly power he sought,
    And Aaron, saint of God, opposed :
Her prey the opening earth has caught,
    And o'er the rash intruder closed.[1]

What means the hateful brand, that springs
    On yon desponding victim's brow ?
'T is great Uzziah's ; 't is the king's :
    All clean of late,—a leper now.

[1] Numb. xvi.

A monarch he with hand profane
 To burn the hallow'd incense chose :
By warning voices check'd in vain,
 Till on his front the plague-spot rose.[1]

What means the record, but to tell
 To ears that hear, and eyes that read,
By that dread doom, which each befell,
 How sinful each presumptuous deed ?
To warn God's people, how they claim
 The honour to his priesthood due ;
Which stamp'd a Monarch's brow with shame,
 By death unknown a Levite slew !

[1] 2 Chron. xxvi.

CXIII

Hymn commendatory of Religious Zeal

WHAT livelier force the hand can sway,
  The heart what holier feel,
Than that which all God's saints obey,
  For God a fervent zeal?

The love of God its ample base,
  Thence springs each godly plan,
Nor aught within its scope has place
  To mar the love of man.

God's glory still it keeps in sight,
  God's will its motions guides;
Truth o'er it sheds a calm clear light,
  And soberness presides.

Such zeal in all thy actions shown,
   Paul, in thy bosom dwelt :
Such zeal, than thou a holier One,
   The Great Exemplar felt.

Fain would we aye his perfect zeal
   With heart sincere ensue ;
Strive what our Saviour felt, to feel,
   And, as He did, to do.

Like Him with zeal the obedient frame,
   As with a cloak, invest ;[1]
And feed the animating flame
   Perennial in the breast.[2]

[1] Isa. lix. 17.   [2] John ii. 17.

CXIV

Hymn condemnatory of False Zeal

ALAS, that vice its guilt should slur
   Beneath religion's mien ;
Or error's cloud-form'd shadows blur
   The light of truth serene !

By Jezebel's feign'd zeal for God
   Was Naboth's ruin plann'd :
Her course was fraud, her means were blood,
   Her end was Naboth's land.[1]

'Come, and my zeal,' proud Jehu cried,
   'See for Jehovah shown !'
But Bethel's calves the boast belied ;
   His aim was Israel's throne.[2]

[1] I Kings xxi.   [2] 2 Kings x.

Zeal for the Lord from John and James
   Fierce words of vengeance drew :
They knew not what their Master's aims,
   Nor what their spirit knew.[1]

The Jews a zeal of God possest ;
   But knowledge with clear light
Was wanted, to inform the breast,
   And guide their steps aright.[2]

Lord, with thy zeal our souls inspire
   To worship at Thy shrine ;
No strange, profane, unhallow'd fire,
   But holy fire of Thine.[3]

A zeal by no intemperance ruled,
   From worldly passions free,
By Thy directing wisdom school'd,
   And sanctified by Thee !

[1] Luke ix. 55, 56.   [2] Rom. x. 2.   [3] Lev. x. 1.

250

CXV

Hymn of General Thanksgiving

O PRAISE we the Lord !
  Vouchsafed her, my soul
For health and for vigour
  Each evening's refreshment

For motion and speech,
  Each blessing bestow'd,
Defence from the terror,
  Nor less from the arrow,

But chiefly we laud
  The signs of Thy love
The bath whence commences
  With strength to enliven,

The truth by Thy Word
  The food at Thy board
The pastors commission'd
  And the Church's communion

My God for each good
her gratitude owes :
each morning renew'd,
of rest and repose.

for hearing and sight,
each ill turn'd away ;
that walketh by night,
that flieth by day.

Thy pledges of grace,
vouchsafed to the soul :
our spiritual race,
to guide, and control :

within us convey'd ;
our sustenance given ;
by Thee for our aid,
to lead us to heaven.

For these, and for all   the gifts of our God,
   To man's sinful race   abundantly shown,
The praise of His bounty   proclaim we abroad,
   His mercy reveal'd for   the sake of His Son.

O praise we the Lord!   To God, who alone
   Is God of our health,   all praise be addrest!
All praise to the Father,   all praise to the Son,
   And the Spirit of goodness,   eternally blest!

CXVI

Hymn commemorative of God's Blessing

WHO would enjoy the highest bliss
  To man in mercy given,
The blessing of our God be his,
  The peace that comes from heaven.

This casts the things of sense behind,
  This lifts the thoughts above,
With heavenly knowledge guards the mind,
  The heart with heavenly love.

Oft as prepares the holy man
  The Church's rites to end,
And bid on her departing train
  ' The peace of God ' descend ;

With bended knees and head inclined,
  And meek and silent prayer,
May we to God's high will resign'd
  His heavenly blessing share.

So may we find in that blest place,
  And, thence departing, keep,
The Father's love, the Son's dear grace,
  The Spirit's fellowship :

So fail not in God's peace to live,
  And with allegiance true
To Father, Son, and Spirit give
  Praise to the Godhead due.

Praise to the Father ; to the Son
  Be praise, the incarnate Word ;
And to the Spirit ; Three and One,
  The Church's God and Lord !

CXVII

Hymn commemoratibe of Sickness

Yes : ' on some fond,' some friendly ' breast
   The parting soul relies ;'
Yet craves she a more lasting rest,
   A Friend above the skies.
In that dread hour from human eyes
   When fades each earthly view,
Rise, O my soul, to God arise,
   And peace with Him ensue !

Oh, then, o'er all bethink thee how
   His mercy-seat to find,
By meek confession's contrite vow,
   With fervent prayer combined ;

By faith to His high will resign'd,
  By penitence profound,
And love for all of human kind
  With fruits of mercy crown'd !

Nor then from hallow'd lips neglect
  The words of peace divine ;
Nor then from hallow'd hands reject
  Salvation's mystic sign :
Nor vain presumptuous thought be thine,
  Nor self-sufficient claim ;
But on Thy Father's love recline,
  And plead Thy Saviour's name.

Thus, O my soul, by sickness prest,
  On God for peace rely ;
Prepared to part, thus seek for rest
  The Holy One and High !

O God, to Thee my soul would fly,
  Her refuge Thee she knows:
O heal her wounds, her wants supply,
  And grant her Thy repose!

CXVIII

Hymn commemorative of Death

God of the spirits of mankind,
As o'er the fading form inclined, ·
We watch a brother's fleeting breath,
Fix in our minds the thought of death !

Oft as the bell with solemn toll
Informs us of a parting soul,
Teach us to think how short the space
Ere ours must quit its resting-place !

When to the earth the corpse we trust,
Ashes to ashes, dust to dust,
Remind us of the coming day
When ours must join its native clay !

R

And when we hear the awful word
That speaks of doom and life restored,
Prompt each to ponder, 'What shall be
That doom, that future life, to me !'

God of our life, whose records give
Thy flock instruction how to live,
That, through Thy Son our sins forgiven,
Our death may be the gate of heaven :

O may each act, when others die,
Prove to ourselves a warning cry,
Advance us on our heavenward road,
And fit us more to meet our God !

CXIX

𝕳𝖞𝖒𝖓 𝖈𝖔𝖒𝖒𝖊𝖒𝖔𝖗𝖆𝖙𝖎𝖛𝖊 𝖔𝖋 𝖆 𝕯𝖊𝖕𝖆𝖗𝖙𝖊𝖉 𝕱𝖗𝖎𝖊𝖓𝖉

AND is thy trial o'er?
　Have all thy hours been told?
And shall we never, never more
　That pleasant face behold?

That sweetly smiling cheek,
　That mildly beaming eye,
Which wont the mind's clear thought to speak,
　The heart's benignity?

And shall we never hear
　Again that cheerful tongue,
On whose soft tones the willing ear
　As on sweet music hung?

Yes ; thou art gone, and we
   Remain behind to tell
How soothing is the thought of thee,
   Beloved so long, so well.

Yet not beyond the scope
   Of faith's keen sight art thou,
As with a ' sure and certain hope,'
   Beside Thy grave we bow :

With certain hope and sure,
   That they, in Christ who rest,
The meek, the merciful, the pure,
   Shall aye in Christ be blest.

Then take our fond regret,
   Withal, dear friend, our trust,
That thou from us art gone to meet
   The assembly of the just.

O come that blissful tide,
When we may worthy prove,
By His dear might for all who died,
To dwell with thee above ![1]

---

[1] These stanzas (and it is probable that the observation may be applied to some others likewise) are perhaps inappropriately called a Hymn. But having been composed whilst this volume was in the press, on intelligence of the death of an old and much valued friend, they are inserted here as agreeing in substance with the other poems with which they are associated.

CXX

Hymn commemorative of the Day of Judgment

O Saviour, awful was the word,
  In Patmos' island lone,
By him in holy vision heard,
  Thy own beloved John.

'Behold! I come, I come with speed:
  With me is my reward:
And then of every man the meed
  Shall with his work accord.'

'Come then!' from every faithful breast
  The Holy Spirit cries;
And 'Come!' in spotless raiment drest,
  The Church, Thy Bride, replies.

O blest are they, whose bosoms share
   The Spirit's gifts serene :
Blest, who the bridal garment wear,
   That vesture white and clean :

Blest, who in Thy communion erst
   Have loved, O Christ, to dwell ;
Have freely drunk and slaked their thirst
   From Thy enlivening well :

And when at length Thy warnings show
   At hand the hour of doom,
Can meekly answer, ' Even so,
   Yea come, Lord Jesus, come !'

INDEX TO THE LATIN HYMNS.

INDEX TO THE ENGLISH HYMNS.

Edinburgh: Printed by Thomas and Archibald Constable,
Printers to the Queen, and to the University.

𝔑𝔢𝔴 𝔚𝔬𝔯𝔨𝔰

IN COURSE OF PUBLICATION BY

Messrs. RIVINGTON,

WATERLOO PLACE, LONDON;

HIGH STREET, OXFORD; TRINITY STREET, CAMBRIDGE.

NOVEMBER, 1870.

DICTIONARY OF DOCTRINAL AND HISTORICAL THEOLOGY.

By VARIOUS WRITERS.

Edited by the Rev. **John Henry Blunt**, M.A., F.S.A., Editor of 'The Annotated Book of Common Prayer.'

One vol., imperial 8vo. 42s.

The Principles of the CATHEDRAL SYSTEM

VINDICATED and FORCED upon MEMBERS of CATHEDRAL FOUNDATIONS.

Eight Sermons, preached in the Cathedral Church of the Holy and Undivided Trinity of Norwich.

By **Edward Meyrick Goulburn**, D.D., Dean of Norwich, late Prebendary of St. Paul's, and one of Her Majesty's Chaplains.

Crown 8vo. 5s.

LONDON, OXFORD, & CAMBRIDGE.

ELEMENTS OF RELIGION.

Lectures delivered at St. James's, Piccadilly, in Lent, 1870.
By **Henry Parry Liddon**, D.C.L., Canon of St. Paul's, and
Ireland Professor of Exegesis in the University of Oxford.
Crown 8vo. [*In the Press.*]

A MANUAL OF LOGIC;

Or, a Statement and Explanation of the Laws of Formal Thought.
By **Henry J. Turrell**, M.A., Oxon.
Square crown 8vo. 2s. 6d.

THE PSALMS translated from the HEBREW.

With Notes, chiefly Exegetical.
By **William Kay**, D.D., Rector of Great Leighs; late Principal of
Bishop's College, Calcutta.
8vo. [*In the Press.*]

SERMONS.

By **Henry Melvill**, B.D., Canon of St. Paul's, and Chaplain
in Ordinary to the Queen.
New Edition. Two vols. Crown 8vo. 5s. each.

THE ORIGIN AND DEVELOPMENT OF
RELIGIOUS BELIEF.

By **S. Baring-Gould**, M.A., Author of 'Curious Myths of the
Middle Ages.'
PART II. CHRISTIANITY. *8vo.* 15s.
PART I. HEATHENISM AND MOSAISM. *8vo.* 15s.

PARISH MUSINGS; or, DEVOTIONAL
POEMS.

By **John S. B. Monsell**, LL.D., Rural Dean, and Rector of
St. Nicholas Guildford.
New Edition. 18mo. Limp cloth, 1s. 6d.; *or in cover,* 1s.

LONDON, OXFORD, & CAMBRIDGE.

THE WITNESS of ST. JOHN to CHRIST;

Being the Boyle Lectures for 1870.

With an Appendix on the Authorship and Integrity of St. John's Gospel and the Unity of the Johannine Writings.

By the Rev. **Stanley Leathes**, M.A., Minister of St. Philip's, Regent Street, and Professor of Hebrew, King's College, London.

8vo.   10s. 6d.

THE ELEGIES OF PROPERTIUS,

Translated into English Verse.

By **Charles Robert Moore**, M.A., late Scholar of Corpus Christi College, Oxford.

Small 8vo.   *[In the Press.*

'THE ATHANASIAN CREED,'

And its Usage in the English Church: an Investigation as to the Original Object of the Creed and the Growth of prevailing Misconceptions regarding it.

A Letter to the Very Reverend W. F. Hook, D.D., F.R.S., Dean of Chichester, from **C. A. Swainson**, D.D., Canon of the Cathedral, and Examining Chaplain to the Lord Bishop of Chichester; Norrisian Professor of Divinity, Cambridge.

Crown 8vo.   3s. 6d.

PRAYERS AND MEDITATIONS FOR THE HOLY COMMUNION.

With a Preface by **C. J. Ellicott**, D.D., Lord Bishop of Gloucester and Bristol.

With Rubrics in red.   Royal 32mo.   2s, 6d.

THE SHEPHERD OF HERMAS.

Translated into English, with an Introduction and Notes.

By **Charles H. Hoole**, M.A., Senior Student of Christ Church, Oxford.

Fcap. 8vo.   4s. 6d.

LONDON, OXFORD, & CAMBRIDGE.

MATERIALS AND MODELS FOR GREEK
AND LATIN PROSE COMPOSITION.

Selected and Arranged by **J. Y. Sargent**, M.A. Tutor, late Fellow of
Magdalen College, Oxford; and **T. F. Dallin**, M.A., Fellow
and Tutor of Queen's College, Oxford.

Crown 8vo. 7s. 6d.

THE STAR OF CHILDHOOD.

A First Book of Prayers and Instruction for Children.

Compiled by a Priest.

Edited by the Rev. **T. T. Carter**, M.A., Rector of Clewer, Berks.

With Illustrations. Royal 16mo. 2s. 6d.

THE DOCTRINE of RECONCILIATION TO
GOD BY JESUS CHRIST.

Seven Lectures, preached during Lent, 1870, with a Prefatory Essay.

By **W. H. Fremantle**, M.A., Rector of St. Mary's, Bryanston Square.

Fcap. 8vo. 2s.

PROGRESSIVE EXERCISES IN LATIN
ELEGIAC VERSE.

By **C. G. Gepp**, B.A., late Junior Student of Christ Church, Oxford,
and Assistant Master at Tonbridge School.

Small 8vo. [*In the Press.*

SELF-RENUNCIATION.

From the French. With Introduction by the Rev. **T. T. Carter**,
M.A., Rector of Clewer.

Crown 8vo. [*In the Press.*

LONDON, OXFORD, & CAMBRIDGE.

THE HIDDEN LIFE OF THE SOUL.

From the French. By the Author of 'A Dominican Artist,' 'Life of Madame Louise de France,' etc., etc.

Crown 8vo. 5s.

ANCIENT HYMNS

From the Roman Breviary. For Domestic Use every Morning and Evening of the Week, and on the Holy Days of the Church.

To which are added, Original Hymns, principally of Commemoration and Thanksgiving for Christ's Holy Ordinances.

By **Richard Mant**, D.D., sometime Lord Bishop of Down and Connor.

New Edition. Small 8vo. 5s. [Nearly ready.

The First Six Books of HOMER'S ODYSSEY.

Edited for the use of Schools, with an Introduction and English Notes by **Henry Musgrave Wilkins**, M.A., Fellow of Merton College, Oxford. .

Crown 8vo. [In preparation.

A HISTORY of the Holy EASTERN CHURCH.

The Patriarchate of Antioch, to the Middle of the Fifth Century.

By the Rev. **John Mason Neale**, D.D., late Warden of Sackville College, East Grinsted.

Followed by a History of the Patriarchs of Antioch, translated from the Greek of Constantius I., Patriarch of Constantinople.

Edited, with an Introduction, by **George Williams**, B.D., Vicar of Ringwood, late Fellow of King's College, Cambridge.

8vo. [In the Press.

ESSAYS ON THE PLATONIC ETHICS.

By **Thomas Maguire**, LL.D. ex S.T.C.D., Professor of Latin, Queen's College, Galway.

8vo. 5s.

ST. JOHN CHRYSOSTOM'S LITURGY.

Translated by **H. C. Romanoff**, Author of 'Sketches of the Rites and Customs of the Greco-Russian Church.'

With Illustrations. Square crown 8vo. [*In the Press.*

THE SAYINGS OF THE GREAT FORTY DAYS,

Between the Resurrection and Ascension, regarded as the Outlines of the Kingdom of God. In Five Discourses. With an Examination of Dr. Newman's Theory of Developments.

By **George Moberly**, D.C.L., Bishop of Salisbury.

Fourth Edition. Uniform with Brighstone Sermons.

Crown 8vo. [*In the Press.*

DEMOSTHENIS ORATIONES PUBLICAE.

Edited by **G. H. Heslop**, M.A., late Fellow and Assistant Tutor of Queen's College, Oxford; Head Master of St. Bees.

Part III. De Falsâ Legatione. Forming a new Part of ' Catena Classicorum.'

Crown 8vo. [*In the Press.*

DEMOSTHENIS ORATIONES PRIVATAE.

Edited by the Rev. **Arthur Holmes**, M.A., Fellow and Lecturer of Clare College, Cambridge; Lecturer and late Fellow of St. John's College,

Part I. De Coronâ. Forming a new Part of 'Catena Classicorum.'

Crown 8vo. [*In the Press.*

THE LIFE OF JUSTIFICATION.

A Series of Lectures delivered in Substance at All Saints', Margaret Street, in Lent, 1870.

By the Rev. **George Body**, B.A., Rector of Kirkby Misperton.

Crown 8vo. [*In the Press.*

LONDON, OXFORD, & CAMBRIDGE.

THE ILIAD OF HOMER.

Translated by **J. G. Cordery**, late of Balliol College, Oxford, and now of H. M. Bengal Civil Service.

Two vols. 8vo.

DICTIONARY OF SECTS, HERESIES,
AND SCHOOLS OF THOUGHT.
By Various Writers.

Edited by the Rev. **John Henry Blunt**, M.A., F.S.A.; Editor of 'The Annotated Book of Common Prayer.'

(FORMING THE SECOND PORTION OF THE 'SUMMARY OF THEOLOGY AND ECCLESIASTICAL HISTORY,' WHICH MESSRS. RIVINGTON HAVE IN COURSE OF PREPARATION AS A 'THESAURUS THEOLOGICUS' FOR THE CLERGY AND LAITY OF THE CHURCH OF ENGLAND.)

Imperial 8vo.   [*In preparation.*

A PLAIN ACCOUNT OF THE ENGLISH
BIBLE,

From the Earliest Times of its Translation to the Present Day.

By **John Henry Blunt**, M.A., Vicar of Kennington, Oxford; Editor of 'The Annotated Book of Common Prayer,' etc.

Crown 8vo. 3s. 6d.

THE POPE AND THE COUNCIL.

By **Janus**. Authorized Translation from the German.

Third Edition, revised. Crown 8vo. 7s. 6d.

The CHURCH of GOD and the BISHOPS:

An Essay suggested by the Convocation of the Vatican Council. By **Henry St. A. Von Liaño**. Authorized Translation.

Crown 8vo. 4s. 6d.

LONDON, OXFORD, & CAMBRIDGE.

LETTERS FROM ROME on the COUNCIL.

By **Quirinus**. Reprinted from the *Allgemeine Zeitung*.
Authorized Translation.

The First Series contains Preliminary History of the Council and
Letters I. to XV.

The Second Series contains Letters XVI. to XXXIV.

Crown 8vo. 3s. 6d. each.

The Third Series, completing the Volume, is just ready.

THE AMMERGAU PASSION PLAY.

Reprinted by permission from the *Times*. With some Introductory
Remarks on the Origin and Development of Miracle Plays,
and some Practical Hints for the use of Intending Visitors.

By the Rev. **Malcolm MacColl**, M.A., Chaplain to the Right Hon.
Lord Napier, K.T.

Second Edition. Crown 8vo. 2s. 6d.

The FIRST BOOK OF COMMON PRAYER

OF EDWARD VI. AND THE ORDINAL OF 1549;

Together with the Order of the Communion, 1548.

Reprinted entire, and Edited by the Rev. **Henry Baskerville Walton**,
M.A., late Fellow and Tutor of Merton College.

With Introduction by the Rev. **Peter Goldsmith Medd**, M.A.,
Senior Fellow and Tutor of University College, Oxford.

Small 8vo. 6s.

THE PURSUIT OF HOLINESS.

A Sequel to 'Thoughts on Personal Religion,' intended to carry the
Reader somewhat farther onward in the Spiritual Life.

By **Edward Meyrick Goulburn**, D.D., Dean of Norwich.

Second Edition. Small 8vo. 5s.

LONDON, OXFORD, & CAMBRIDGE.

APOSTOLICAL SUCCESSION IN THE CHURCH OF ENGLAND.

By the Rev. **Arthur W. Haddan**, B.D., Rector of Barton-on-the-Heath, and late Fellow of Trinity College, Oxford.

8vo. 12*s.*

THE PRIEST TO THE ALTAR;

Or, Aids to the Devout Celebration of Holy Communion; chiefly after the Ancient Use of Sarum.

Second Edition. Enlarged, Revised, and Re-arranged with the Secretæ, Post-communion, etc., appended to the Collects, Epistles, and Gospels, throughout the Year.

8vo. 7*s.* 6*d.*

NEWMAN'S (J. H.) PAROCHIAL AND PLAIN SERMONS.

Edited by the Rev. **W. J. Copeland**, Rector of Farnham, Essex.

From the Text of the last Editions published by Messrs. Rivington.

Eight vols. *Crown 8vo.* 5*s. each.*

NEWMAN'S (J. H.) SERMONS, BEARING UPON SUBJECTS OF THE DAY.

Edited by the Rev. **W. J. Copeland**, Rector of Farnham, Essex.

From the Text of the last Edition published by Messrs. Rivington. With Index of Dates of all the Sermons.

Printed uniformly with the 'Parochial and Plain Sermons.'

Crown 8vo. 5*s.*

BRIGHSTONE SERMONS.

By **George Moberly**, D.C.L., Bishop of Salisbury.

Second Edition. *Crown 8vo.* 7*s.* 6*d.*

LONDON, OXFORD, & CAMBRIDGE.

The CHARACTERS of the OLD TESTAMENT.

In a Series of Sermons.

By the Rev. **Isaac Williams**, B.D., late Fellow of Trinity College, Oxford.

New Edition. Crown 8vo. 5s.

FEMALE CHARACTERS of HOLY SCRIPTURE.

In a Series of Sermons.

By the Rev. **Isaac Williams**, B.D., late Fellow of Trinity College, Oxford.

New Edition. Crown 8vo. 5s.

THE DIVINITY OF OUR LORD AND SAVIOUR JESUS CHRIST:

Being the Bampton Lectures for 1866.

By **Henry Parry Liddon**, D.C.L., Canon of St. Paul's, and Ireland Professor of Exegesis in the University of Oxford.

Fourth Edition. Crown 8vo. 5s.

SERMONS PREACHED BEFORE THE UNIVERSITY OF OXFORD.

By **Henry Parry Liddon**, D.C.L., Canon of St. Paul's, and Ireland Professor of Exegesis in the University of Oxford.

Third Edition, revised. Crown 8vo. 5s.

A MANUAL FOR THE SICK;

With other Devotions.

By **Launcelot Andrewes**, D.D., sometime Lord Bishop of Winchester.

Edited, with a Preface, by **Henry Parry Liddon**, D.C.L., Canon of St. Paul's.

With Portrait. Second Edition. Large type. 24mo. 2s. 6d.

WALTER KERR HAMILTON: BISHOP of SALISBURY.

A Sketch, Reprinted, with Additions and Corrections, from
the *Guardian.*

By **Henry Parry Liddon,** D.C.L., Canon of St. Paul's.

Second Edition. 8vo. Limp cloth, 2s. 6d.

Or, bound with the Sermon, 'Life in Death,' *3s. 6d.*

THE LIFE OF MADAME LOUISE DE FRANCE,

Daughter of Louis XV., also known as the Mother Térèse de
S. Augustin. By the Author of ' Tales of Kirkbeck.'

Crown 8vo. 6s.

JOHN WESLEY'S PLACE IN CHURCH HISTORY DETERMINED,

With the aid of Facts and Documents unknown to, or unnoticed
by, his Biographers.

With a New and Authentic Portrait.

By **R. Denny Urlin,** M.R.I.A., of the Middle Temple,
Barrister-at-Law.

Small 8vo. 5s. 6d.

THE TREASURY OF DEVOTION:

A Manual of Prayers for General and Daily Use.

Compiled by a Priest. Edited by the Rev. **T. T. Carter,** M.A.,
Rector of Clewer, Berks.

Third Edition. 16mo, limp cloth 2s.; cloth extra, 2s. 6d.

Bound with the Book of Common Prayer, *3s. 6d.*

LONDON, OXFORD, & CAMBRIDGE.

THE GUIDE TO HEAVEN:

A Book of Prayers for every Want. (For the Working Classes.)
Compiled by a Priest. Edited by the Rev. **T. T. Carter**, M.A.,
Rector of Clewer, Berks.

Crown 8vo, limp cloth, 1s. ; cloth extra, 1s. 6d.

A DOMINICAN ARTIST :

A Sketch of the Life of the Rev. Père Besson, of the Order of
St. Dominic.

By the Author of 'Tales of Kirkbeck,' 'The Life of
Madame Louise de France,' etc.

Crown 8vo. 9s.

THE REFORMATION OF THE CHURCH OF ENGLAND;

Its History, Principles, and Results. A.D. 1514-1547.

By **John Henry Blunt**, M.A., Vicar of Kennington, Oxford, Editor
of 'The Annotated Book of Common Prayer,' Author of
'Directorium Pastorale,' etc., etc.

Second Edition. 8vo. 16s.

THE VIRGIN'S LAMP:

Prayers and Devout Exercises for English Sisters, chiefly composed
and selected by the late Rev. **J. M. Neale**, D.D., Founder of
St. Margaret's, East Grinsted.

Small 8vo. 3s. 6d.

CATECHETICAL NOTES AND CLASS QUESTIONS, LITERAL & MYSTICAL;

Chiefly on the Earlier Books of Holy Scripture.

By the late Rev. **J. M. Neale**, D.D., Warden of Sackville College,
East Grinsted.

Crown 8vo. 5s.

LONDON, OXFORD, & CAMBRIDGE.

SERMONS FOR CHILDREN:

Being Thirty-three short Readings, addressed to the Children of
St. Margaret's Home, East Grinsted.

By the late Rev. **J. M. Neale**, D.D., Warden of Sackville College.

Second Edition. Small 8vo. 3s. 6d.

THE WITNESS of the OLD TESTAMENT TO CHRIST.

The Boyle Lectures for the Year 1868.

By the Rev. **Stanley Leathes**, M.A., Professor of Hebrew in King's
College, London, and Minister of St. Philip's, Regent Street.

8vo. 9s.

THE WITNESS of ST. PAUL to CHRIST:

Being the Boyle Lectures for 1869.

With an Appendix, on the Credibility of the Acts, in Reply to
the Recent Strictures of Dr. Davidson.

By the Rev. **Stanley Leathes**, M.A., Professor of Hebrew in King's
College, London, and Minister of St. Philip's, Regent Street.

8vo. 10s. 6d.

HONORÉ DE BALZAC.

Edited, with English Notes and Introductory Notice, by **Henri Van
Laun**, formerly French Master at Cheltenham College, and
now Master of the French Language and Literature at
the Edinburgh Academy.

(BEING THE FIRST VOLUME OF 'SELECTIONS FROM MODERN FRENCH AUTHORS.')

Crown 8vo. 3s. 6d.

H. A. TAINE.

Edited, with English Notes and Introductory Notice, by **Henri Van Laun**, formerly French Master at Cheltenham College, and now Master of the French Language and Literature at the Edinburgh Academy.

(BEING THE SECOND VOLUME OF 'SELECTIONS FROM MODERN FRENCH AUTHORS.')

Crown 8vo. 3s. 6d.

DEAN ALFORD'S GREEK TESTAMENT.

With English Notes, intended for the Upper Forms of Schools, and for Pass-men at the Universities.

Abridged by **Bradley H. Alford**, M.A., late Scholar of Trinity College, Cambridge.

Crown 8vo. 10s. 6d.

ELEMENTARY ALGEBRA.

By **J. Hamblin Smith**, M.A, Gonville and Caius College, and Lecturer at St. Peter's College, Cambridge.

New Edition, Revised and Enlarged. Crown 8vo. 4s. 6d.

ELEMENTARY TRIGONOMETRY.

By **J. Hamblin Smith**, M.A., Gonville and Caius College, and Lecturer at St. Peter's College, Cambridge.

Third Edition, Revised and Enlarged. Crown 8vo. 4s. 6d.

ELEMENTARY STATICS,

By **J. Hamblin Smith**, M.A., Gonville and Caius College, and Lecturer at St. Peter's College, Cambridge.

Royal 8vo. 5s.

ELEMENTARY HYDROSTATICS.

By **J. Hamblin Smith**, M.A., Gonville and Caius College, and
Lecturer at St. Peter's College, Cambridge.

Second Edition, Revised and Enlarged.   *Crown 8vo.*   3s.

EXERCISES ADAPTED TO ALGEBRA.

PART I.

By **J. Hamblin Smith**, M.A., Gonville and Caius College; and
Lecturer at St. Peter's College, Cambridge.

Crown 8vo.   2s. 6d.

ELEMENTS OF EUCLID,

Arranged with the Abbreviations admitted in the Cambridge
Examinations, and with Exercises.

By **J. Hamblin Smith**, M.A., Gonville and Caius College; and
Lecturer at St. Peter's College, Cambridge.

Crown 8vo.   [*In the Press.*

ARITHMETIC, THEORETICAL AND PRACTICAL.

By **W. H. Girdlestone**, M.A., of Christ's College, Cambridge,
Principal of the Theological College, Gloucester.

New and Revised Edition.   Crown 8vo.   6s. 6d.

Also an Edition for Schools.   *Small 8vo.*   3s. 6d.

CLASSICAL EXAMINATION PAPERS.

Edited, with Notes and References, by **P. J. F. Gantillon**, M.A.,
sometime Scholar of St. John's College, Cambridge;
Classical Master in Cheltenham College.

Crown 8vo.   7s. 6d.   *Or interleaved with writing-paper for Notes,
half-bound,* 10s. 6d.

LONDON, OXFORD, & CAMBRIDGE.

THE STORY OF THE GOSPELS.

In a single Narrative, combined from the Four Evangelists, showing
in a new translation their unity. To which is added, a like
continuous narrative in the Original Greek.

By the Rev. **William Pound**, M.A., late Fellow of St. John's College,
Cambridge; Principal of Appulddurcombe School,
Isle of Wight.

Two vols. 8vo. 36s.

THE LYRICS OF HORACE,

Done into English Rhyme.

By **Thomas Charles Baring**, M.A., late Fellow of Brasenose College,
Oxford.

Small 4to. 7s.

A PLAIN AND SHORT HISTORY OF ENGLAND FOR CHILDREN.

In Letters from a Father to his Son. With a Set of Questions
at the end of each Letter.

By **George Davys**, D.D., late Bishop of Peterborough.

New Edition, with Twelve Coloured Illustrations.

Square Crown 8vo. 3s. 6d.

A Cheap Edition for Schools, with portrait of Edward VI.

18mo. 1s. 6d.

HISTORY OF THE COLLEGE OF ST. JOHN THE EVANGELIST, CAMBRIDGE.

By **Thomas Baker**, B.D., Ejected Fellow.

Edited for the Syndics of the University Press, by **John E. B. Mayor**,
M.A., Fellow of St. John's College.

Two vols. 8vo. 24s.

MEMOIR OF THE RIGHT REV. JOHN
STRACHAN, *D.D., LL.D., First Bishop of Toronto.*

By **A. N. Bethune**, D.D., D.C.L., his Successor in the See.

8vo. 10s.

THE PRAYER BOOK INTERLEAVED;

With Historical Illustrations and Explanatory Notes arranged
parallel to the Text.

By the Rev. **W. M. Campion**, D.D., Fellow and Tutor of Queen's
College, and Rector of St. Botolph's, and the Rev. **W. J. Beamont**,
M.A., late Fellow of Trinity College, Cambridge.

With a Preface by the **Lord Bishop of Ely.**

Fifth Edition. Small 8vo. 7s. 6d.

CONSOLING THOUGHTS IN SICKNESS.

Edited by **Henry Bailey**, B.D., Warden of St. Augustine's College,
Canterbury.

Large type. Fine Edition. Small 8vo. 2s. 6d.

Also a Cheap Edition, 1s. 6d.; or in paper cover, 1s.

SICKNESS; ITS TRIALS & BLESSINGS.

New Edition, Small 8vo. 3s. 6d.

Also a Cheap Edition, 1s. 6d.; or in paper cover, 1s.

HYMNS AND POEMS FOR THE SICK
AND SUFFERING;

In connection with the Service for the Visitation of the Sick.
Selected from various Authors.

Edited by **T. V. Fosbery**, M.A., Vicar of St. Giles's, Reading.

New Edition. Small 8vo. 3s. 6d.

LONDON, OXFORD, & CAMBRIDGE.

HELP AND COMFORT FOR THE SICK
POOR.

By the Author of ' Sickness; its Trials and Blessings.'

New Edition. Small 8vo. 1s.

THE DOGMATIC FAITH:

An Inquiry into the relation subsisting between Revelation and
Dogma. Being the Bampton Lectures for 1867.

By **Edward Garbett**, M.A., Incumbent of Christ Church, Surbiton.

Second Edition. Crown 8vo. 7s. 6d.

SKETCHES OF THE RITES & CUSTOMS
OF THE GRECO-RUSSIAN CHURCH.

By **H. C. Romanoff.** With an Introductory Notice by the Author
of ' The Heir of Redclyffe.'

Second Edition. Crown 8vo. 7s. 6d.

HOUSEHOLD THEOLOGY:

A Handbook of Religious Information respecting the Holy Bible,
the Prayer Book, the Church, the Ministry, Divine Worship,
the Creeds, etc., etc.

By **John Henry Blunt**, M.A.

Third Edition. Small 8vo. 3s. 6d.

CURIOUS MYTHS OF THE MIDDLE
AGES.

By **S. Baring-Gould**, M.A., Author of ' Post-Mediæval Preachers,'
etc. With Illustrations.

Complete in one Volume.

New Edition. Crown 8vo. 6s.

LONDON, OXFORD, & CAMBRIDGE.

SOI-MÊME; a Story of a Wilful Life.
Small 8vo. 3s. 6d.

THE HAPPINESS OF THE BLESSED,

Considered as to the Particulars of their State: their Recognition of each other in that State: and its Differences of Degrees.

To which are added, Musings on the Church and her Services.

By **Richard Mant**, D.D., sometime Lord Bishop of Down & Connor.

New Edition. Small 8vo. 3s. 6d.

THE HOLY BIBLE.
With Notes and Introductions.
By **Chr. Wordsworth**, D.D., Bishop of Lincoln.
Imperial 8vo.

VOLUME I. 38s.

PART		£	s.	d.
I. Genesis and Exodus. *Second Edition* . . .		1	1	0
II. Leviticus, Numbers, Deuteronomy. *Second Edit.*		0	18	0

VOLUME II. 21s.

		£	s.	d.
III. Joshua, Judges, Ruth. *Second Edition* . .		0	12	0
IV. The Book of Samuel. *Second Edition* . .		0	10	0

VOLUME III. 21s.

		£	s.	d.
V. The Books of Kings, Chronicles, Ezra, Nehemiah, Esther. *Second Edition* . . .		1	1	0

VOLUME IV. 34s.

		£	s.	d.
VI. The Book of Job. *Second Edition* . .		0	9	0
VII. The Book of Psalms. *Second Edition* . .		0	15	0
VIII. Proverbs, Ecclesiastes, Song of Solomon .		0	12	0

VOLUME V. 32s. 6d.

		£	s.	d.
IX. Isaiah		0	12	6
X. Jeremiah, Lamentations, and Ezekiel . .		1	1	0

VOLUME VI.

		£	s.	d.
XI. Daniel. (*In Preparation.*)				
XII. The Minor Prophets		0	12	0

LONDON, OXFORD, & CAMBRIDGE.

MISCELLANEOUS POEMS.

By **Henry Francis Lyte**, M.A.

New Edition.   Small 8vo.   5s.

PERRANZABULOE, THE LOST CHURCH
FOUND;

Or, The Church of England not a New Church, but Ancient, Apostolical, and Independent, and a Protesting Church Nine Hundred Years before the Reformation.

By the **Rev. C. T. Collins Trelawny**, M.A., formerly Rector of Timsbury, Somerset, and late Fellow of Balliol College, Oxford.

With Illustrations.   New Edition.   Crown 8vo.   3s. 6d.

CATECHESIS; *or,* CHRISTIAN INSTRUCTION

Preparatory to Confirmation and First Communion.

By **Charles Wordsworth**, D.C.L., Bishop of St. Andrew's.

New Edition.   Small 8vo.   2s.

WARNINGS OF THE HOLY WEEK, *etc.;*

Being a Course of Parochial Lectures for the Week before Easter and the Easter Festivals.

By the **Rev. W. Adams**, M.A., late Vicar of St. Peter's-in-the-East, Oxford, and Fellow of Merton College.

Sixth Edition.   Small 8vo.   4s. 6d.

CONSOLATIO; OR, COMFORT FOR THE
AFFLICTED.

Edited by the Rev. **C. E. Kennaway.**   With a Preface by **Samuel Wilberforce**, D.D., Lord Bishop of Winchester.

New Edition.   Small 8vo.   3s. 6d.

THE HILLFORD CONFIRMATION: a Tale.

By **M. C. Phillpotts.**

18*mo.* 1*s.*

FROM MORNING TO EVENING:

A Book for Invalids.

From the French of M. L'Abbé Henri Perreyve.

Translated and adapted by an Associate of the Sisterhood of
S. John Baptist, Clewer.

Crown 8vo. 5*s.*

FAMILY PRAYERS;

Compiled from Various Sources (chiefly from Bishop Hamilton's
Manual), and arranged on the Liturgical Principle.

By **Edward Meyrick Goulburn**, D.D., Dean of Norwich.

New Edition.   Crown 8vo, large type, 3*s.* 6*d.*

Cheap Edition. 16*mo.* 1*s.*

THE ANNUAL REGISTER:

A Review of Public Events at Home and Abroad, for the Year 1869 ;
being the Seventh Volume of an Improved Series.

8*vo.* 18*s.*

⁎⁎⁎ The Volumes for 1863 *to* 1868 *may be had, price* 18*s. each.*

A PROSE TRANSLATION OF VIRGIL'S
ECLOGUES AND GEORGICS.

By an Oxford Graduate.

Crown 8vo. 2*s.* 6*d.*

LONDON, OXFORD, & CAMBRIDGE.

THE CAMBRIDGE PARAGRAPH BIBLE
OF THE AUTHORIZED ENGLISH VERSION.

With the Text Revised by a Collation of its Early and other
Principal Editions, the Use of the Italic type made Uniform,
the Marginal References Re-modelled, and a Critical
Introduction prefixed.

By the Rev. **F. H. Scrivener**, M.A., Rector of St. Gerrans; Editor
of the Greek Testament, Codex Augiensis, etc.   Edited
for the Syndics of the University Press.

Crown 4to.

Part I., Genesis to Solomon's Song, 15*s.*

Part II., Apocrypha and New Testament, 15*s.*

To be completed in Three Parts.

Part III., Prophetical Books, will be ready about May, 1871.

*** A small number of copies has also been printed, on *good
writing paper*, with one column of print and wide margin to
each page for MS. notes. *Part I., 20s.; Part II., 20s.*

QUIET MOMENTS:

A Four Weeks' Course of Thoughts and Meditations,
before Evening Prayer and at Sunset.

By Lady Charlotte Maria Pepys.

New Edition.   Small 8vo.   2s. 6d.

MORNING NOTES OF PRAISE:

A Series of Meditations upon the Morning Psalms.

By Lady Charlotte Maria Pepys.

New Edition.   Small 8vo.   2s. 6d.

LONDON, OXFORD, & CAMBRIDGE.

YESTERDAY, TO-DAY, AND FOR EVER;

A Poem in Twelve Books.

By **Edward Henry Bickersteth**, M.A., vicar of Christ Church, Hampstead, and Chaplain to the Bishop of Ripon.

Fourth Edition. Small 8vo. 6s.

THE COMMENTARIES OF GAIUS:

Translated, with Notes, by **J. T. Abdy**, LL.D., Regius Professor of Laws in the University of Cambridge, and Barrister-at-Law of the Norfolk Circuit: formerly Fellow of Trinity Hall; and **Bryan Walker**, M.A., M.L.; Fellow and Lecturer of Corpus Christi College, and Law Lecturer of St. John's College, Cambridge; formerly Law Student of Trinity Hall and Chancellor's Legal Medallist.

Crown 8vo. 12s. 6d.

SACRED ALLEGORIES:

The Shadow of the Cross—The Distant Hills—The Old Man's Home—The King's Messengers.

By the Rev. **W. Adams**, M.A., late Fellow of Merton College, Oxford.

Presentation Edition. With Engravings from original designs by Charles W. Cope, R.A., John C. Horsley, A.R.A., Samuel Palmer, Birket Foster, and George Hicks.

Small 4to. 10s. 6d.

The Four Allegories, separately. *Crown 8vo. 2s. 6d. each.*

HERBERT TRESHAM:

A Tale of the Great Rebellion.

By the late Rev. **J. M. Neale**, D.D., sometime Scholar of Trinity College, Cambridge, and late Warden of Sackville College, East Grinsted.

New Edition. Small 8vo. 3s. 6d.

THE MANOR FARM: a Tale.

By **M. C. Phillpotts**, Author of 'The Hillford Confirmation.'

With Four Illustrations. Small 8vo. 3s. 6d.

LONDON, OXFORD, & CAMBRIDGE.

23

LIBER PRECUM PUBLICARUM
ECCLESIÆ ANGLICANÆ.

A **Gulielmo Bright**, A.M., et **Petro Goldsmith Medd**, A.M.,
Presbyteris, Collegii Universitatis in Acad. Oxon.
Sociis, Latine redditus.

New Edition, with all the Rubrics in red.   Small 8vo.   6s.

BIBLE READINGS FOR FAMILY PRAYER.

By the Rev. **W. H. Ridley**, M.A., Rector of Hambleden.

Crown 8vo.

Old Testament—Genesis and Exodus.   2*s.*

New Testament, 3*s.* 6*d.*   { St. Matthew and St. Mark.   2*s.*
{ St. Luke and St. John.   2*s.*

INSTRUCTIONS FOR THE USE OF
CANDIDATES FOR HOLY ORDERS,

And of the Parochial Clergy; with Acts of Parliament relating to
the same, and Forms proposed to be used.

By **Christopher Hodgson**, M.A., Secretary to the Governors of
Queen Anne's Bounty.

Ninth Edition, Revised and Enlarged, 8vo.   16s.

ENGLAND RENDERED IMPREGNABLE

By the practical Military Organization and efficient Equipment of her
National Forces; and her Present Position, Armament, Coast
Defences, Administration, and Future Power considered.

By **H. A. L.**, 'The Old Shekarry.'

8vo.   [*Nearly ready.*

CATENA CLASSICORUM:

A SERIES OF CLASSICAL AUTHORS,

EDITED BY MEMBERS OF BOTH UNIVERSITIES UNDER THE DIRECTION OF

THE REV. ARTHUR HOLMES, M.A.,

Fellow and Lecturer of Clare College, Cambridge, Lecturer and Late Fellow of St. John's College;

AND

THE REV. CHARLES BIGG, M.A.,

Late Senior Student and Tutor of Christ Church, Oxford, Second Classical Master of Cheltenham College.

Crown 8vo.

THE FOLLOWING PARTS HAVE BEEN ALREADY PUBLISHED :—

SOPHOCLIS TRAGOEDIAE.

Edited by R. C. JEBB, M.A., Fellow and Assistant Tutor of Trinity College, Cambridge, and Public Orator of the University.
The Electra, 3*s.* 6*d.*   The Ajax, 3*s.* 6*d.*

JUVENALIS SATIRAE.

Edited by G. A. SIMCOX, M.A., Fellow and Classical Lecturer of Queen's College, Oxford.
3*s.* 6*d.*

THUCYDIDIS HISTORIA.

Edited by CHARLES BIGG, M.A, late Senior Student and Tutor of Christ Church, Oxford.   Second Classical Master of Cheltenham College.
Books I. and II. with Introductions.   6*s.*

LONDON, OXFORD, & CAMBRIDGE.

DEMOSTHENIS ORATIONES PUBLICAE.

Edited by G. H. HESLOP, M.A., Late Fellow and Assistant Tutor of Queen's College, Oxford. Head Master of St. Bees.

The Olynthiacs and the Philippics. 4*s.* 6*d.*

ARISTOPHANIS COMOEDIAE.

Edited by W. C. GREEN, M.A., late Fellow of King's College, Cambridge. Classical Lecturer at Queen's College.

The Acharnians and the Knights. 4*s.*
The Clouds. 3*s.* 6*d.*
The Wasps. 3*s.* 6*d.*

An Edition of the Archarnians and the Knights, Revised and especially adapted for Use in Schools. 4*s.*

ISOCRATIS ORATIONES.

Edited by JOHN EDWIN SANDYS, M.A., Fellow and Tutor of St. John's College, and Classical Lecturer at Jesus College, Cambridge.

Ad Demonicum et Panegyricus. 4*s.* 6*d.*

PERSII SATIRAE.

Edited by A. PRETOR, M.A., of Trinity College, Cambridge, Classical Lecturer of Trinity Hall. 3*s.* 6*d.*

HOMERI ILIAS.

Edited by S. H. REYNOLDS, M.A., Fellow and Tutor of Brasenose College, Oxford.

Books I. to XII. 6*s.*

TERENTI COMOEDIAE.

Edited by T. L. PAPILLON, M.A., Fellow and Classical Lecturer of Merton College, Oxford.

Andria et Eunuchus. 4*s.* 6*d.*

KEYS TO CHRISTIAN KNOWLEDGE.

Small 8vo.   2s. 6d. each.

A KEY TO THE KNOWLEDGE AND USE OF THE BOOK OF COMMON PRAYER.

By **John Henry Blunt,** M.A.

A KEY TO THE KNOWLEDGE AND USE OF THE HOLY BIBLE.

By **John Henry Blunt,** M.A.

A KEY TO THE KNOWLEDGE OF CHURCH HISTORY (ANCIENT).

Edited by **John Henry Blunt,** M.A.

A KEY TO THE NARRATIVE OF THE FOUR GOSPELS.

By **John Pilkington Norris,** M.A., Canon of Bristol, formerly one of Her Majesty's Inspectors of Schools.

A KEY TO THE KNOWLEDGE OF CHURCH HISTORY (MODERN).

Edited by **John Henry Blunt,** M.A.

A KEY TO CHRISTIAN DOCTRINE & PRACTICE.

(Founded on the Church Catechism.)

By **John Henry Blunt,** M.A.

LONDON, OXFORD, & CAMBRIDGE.

RIVINGTON'S DEVOTIONAL SERIES.

Elegantly printed with red borders. 16mo. 2s. 6d.

THOMAS À KEMPIS, OF THE IMITATION OF CHRIST.

Also a cheap Edition, without the red borders, 1s., or in Cover, 6d.

THE RULE AND EXERCISES OF HOLY LIVING.

By **Jeremy Taylor**, D.D., Bishop of Down, and Connor, and Dromore.

Also a cheap Edition, without the red borders, 1s.

THE RULE AND EXERCISES OF HOLY DYING.

By **Jeremy Taylor**, D.D., Bishop of Down, and Connor, and Dromore.

Also a cheap Edition, without the red borders, 1s.

⁎⁎ The 'Holy Living' and the 'Holy Dying' may be had bound together in One Volume, 5s., or without the red borders, 2s. 6d.

A SHORT AND PLAIN INSTRUCTION

For the better Understanding of the Lord's Supper; to which is annexed, the Office of the Holy Communion, with proper Helps and Directions.

By **Thomas Wilson,** D.D., late Lord Bishop of Sodor and Man.

Complete Edition, in large type.

Also a cheap Edition, without the red borders, 1s., or in Cover, 6d.

INTRODUCTION TO THE DEVOUT LIFE.

From the French of St. Francis of Sales, Bishop and Prince of Geneva. A New Translation.

A PRACTICAL TREATISE CONCERNING EVIL THOUGHTS.

By **William Chilcot**, M.A.

ENGLISH POEMS AND PROVERBS.

By **George Herbert.**

LONDON, OXFORD, & CAMBRIDGE.

THE 'ASCETIC LIBRARY:'

A Series of Translations of Spiritual Works for Devotional
Reading from Catholic Sources.

Edited by the Rev. **Orby Shipley**, M.A.

Square Crown 8vo.

THE MYSTERIES OF MOUNT CALVARY.

Translated from the Latin of **Antonio de Guevara.** 3*s.* 6*d.*

PREPARATION FOR DEATH.

Translated from the Italian of **Alfonso**, Bishop of S. Agatha. 5*s.*

COUNSELS ON HOLINESS OF LIFE.

Translated from the Spanish of 'The Sinner's Guide' by
Luis de Granada. 5*s.*

EXAMINATION OF CONSCIENCE UPON SPECIAL SUBJECTS.

Translated and Abridged from the French of **Tronson.** 5*s.*

LONDON, OXFORD, & CAMBRIDGE.

NEW PAMPHLETS.

BY ARCHDEACON BICKERSTETH.

A CHARGE,

Delivered at his Eleventh Visitation of the Archdeaconry of
Buckingham, in May and June, 1870.

8vo. 1s.

THE RESURRECTION OF THE BODY:

A Sermon, preached in the Parish Church of Horsendon, on the
Second Sunday after Easter, 1870, on the occasion of the
Death of Lucy Olivia Hobart, wife of the Rev.
W. E. Partridge, of Horsendon House, Bucks.

8vo. 1s.

BY THE REV. F. GARDEN.

CAN AN ORDAINED MAN BECOME A LAYMAN?

Some Remarks on Mr. Herbert's Bill.

8vo. 6d.

THE ARNOLD HISTORICAL ESSAY, 1870.

THE SCYTHIC NATIONS,

Down to the Fall of the Western Empire.
By JOHN GENT, B.A., Fellow of Trinity College, Oxford.

8vo. 2s.

BY THE REV. A. PERCEVAL PUREY CUST.

OUR COMMON FRAILTY:

A Sermon, preached in the Parish Church of St. Lawrence, Reading,
on Quinquagesima Sunday, February 27, 1870, at the
Opening of the Spring Assize.

8vo. 6d.

BY THE REV. W. B. GALLOWAY.

'OUR HOLY AND OUR BEAUTIFUL HOUSE.'

A Sermon preached at Dunstable, on Sunday, May 22, 1870, on
behalf of the Restoration of Dunstable Church.

8vo. 6d.

LONDON, OXFORD, & CAMBRIDGE.

Ne w Pamphlets—*continued.*

BY THE RIGHT HON. SIR ROBERT PHILLIMORE, D.C.L.

JUDGMENT,

Delivered by The Right Hon. Sir Robert Phillimore, D.C.L., Official Principal of the Arches Court of Canterbury, in the case of the Office of the Judge promoted by Sheppard *v.* Bennett.

Edited by Walter G. F. Phillimore, B.C.L., of the Middle Temple, Barrister-at-Law; Fellow of All Souls' College, and Vinerian Scholar, Oxford.

8vo. 2s. 6d.

BY CANON LIDDON.

PAUPERISM AND THE LOVE OF GOD:

A Sermon, preached at St. Paul's, Knightsbridge, on the Second Sunday after Trinity, 1870, for the Convalescent Hospital at Ascot.

8vo. 1s.

HOW TO DO GOOD:

A Sermon, preached in the Cathedral Church of St. Paul, May 18, 1870, at the Two Hundred and Sixteenth Anniversary Festival of the Sons of the Clergy.

8vo. 6d.

THE MODEL OF OUR NEW LIFE.

A Sermon, preached at the Special Evening Service in St. Paul's Cathedral on Easter Day, 1870.

8vo. 3d., or 2s. 6d. per dozen.

BY THE REV. E. H. BICKERSTETH.

JESUS AND THE RESURRECTION;

Or, the Ministry of the Church a Witness for the Resurrection. A Paper read before the Diocesan Conference of Clergy in the Convocation House, Oxford, July, 1869.

8vo. 6d.

BY CANON BRIGHT.

CHRIST'S PRESENCE AMID THEOLOGICAL STUDIES.

A Sermon, preached in the Parish Church of Cuddesdon, on the Anniversary Festival of Cuddesdon College, June 14, 1870.

8vo. 6d.

Eight Volumes, Crown 8vo, 5s. each.

A New and Uniform Edition of

A DEVOTIONAL · COMMENTARY

ON THE

GOSPEL NARRATIVE.

BY THE

Rev. ISAAC WILLIAMS, B.D.

FORMERLY FELLOW OF TRINITY COLLEGE, OXFORD.

—oo—

THOUGHTS ON THE STUDY OF THE HOLY GOSPELS.

Characteristic Differences in the Four Gospels—Our Lord's Manifestations of Himself—The Rule of Scriptural Interpretation Furnished by Our Lord —Analogies of the Gospel—Mention of Angels in the Gospels—Places of Our Lord's Abode and Ministry—Our Lord's Mode of Dealing with His Apostles—Conclusion.

A HARMONY OF THE FOUR EVANGELISTS.

Our Lord's Nativity—Our Lord's Ministry (Second Year)—Our Lord's Ministry (Third Year)—The Holy Week—Our Lord's Passion—Our Lord's Resurrection.

OUR LORD'S NATIVITY.

The Birth at Bethlehem—The Baptism in Jordan—The First Passover.

OUR LORD'S MINISTRY. SECOND YEAR.

The Second Passover—Christ with the Twelve—The Twelve sent Forth.

· OUR LORD'S MINISTRY. THIRD YEAR.

Teaching in Galilee—Teaching at Jerusalem—Last Journey from Galilee to Jerusalem.

THE HOLY WEEK.

The Approach to Jerusalem—The Teaching in the Temple—The Discourse on the Mount of Olives—The Last Supper.

OUR LORD'S PASSION.

The Hour of Darkness—The Agony—The Apprehension—The Condemnation— The Day of Sorrows—The Hall of Judgment—The Crucifixion—The Sepulture.

OUR LORD'S RESURRECTION.

The Day of Days—The Grave Visited—Christ Appearing—The Going to Emmaus — The Forty Days—The Apostles Assembled — The Lake in Galilee—The Mountain in Galilee—The Return from Galilee.

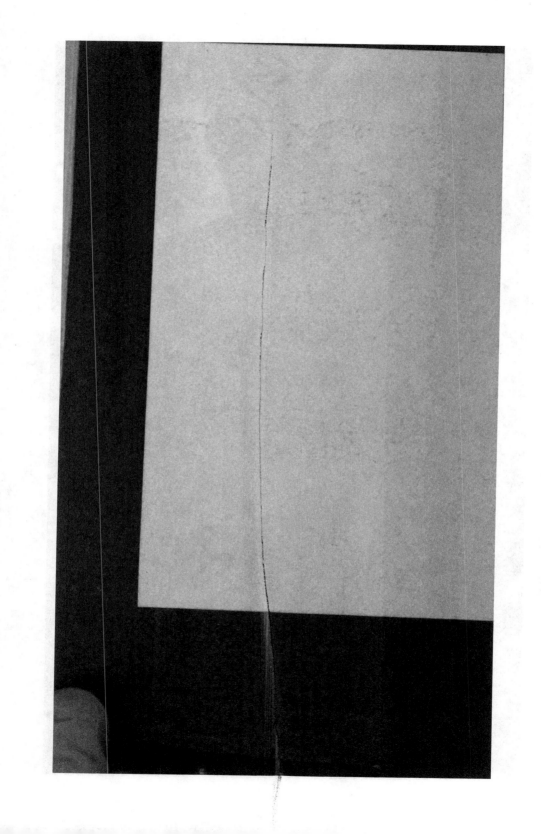

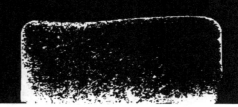